D1695324

BEIJING

北京

中国旅游出版社
China Travel & Tourism Press

特别提示：

"欣赏古都风貌，聆听文化之声"是我们新版《北京》画册带给您的绝对与众不同的享受。

翻开册页，您不仅能领略到精美摄影作品带给您的视觉盛宴，而且，由于添加了"妙笔"音频信息，还能给您带来视听兼具、足以心动的双重体验。

您只要使用"爱国者妙笔"先点击本画册封面右下角的"⊙"标识，再选择画册内您所观赏页面中的"⊙"标识，即可听到本页图片背后的文化故事。

Special Instruction

"Appreciating the charm of old capital and listening to the voice of culture" is the distinguishing pleasure the newly-published Beijing is designed to give.

Open this book, the readers can not only enjoy a feast of gorgeous photographs of Beijing, but also experience the sound effect that touches the very bottom of their hearts.

Use aigopen to press button "⊙" at the right bottom of the cover and choose sign "⊙", you can hear about the story behind those pictures.

妙笔使用说明：

按妙笔"⊙▶‖"键3秒开（关）机，点击封面右下角的"⊙"标识，让妙笔带您欣赏东方古都——北京的古今风采。

用妙笔点触每幅图片中的"⊙"图标，即可倾听这幅美妙景物背后的文化故事。

短按妙笔"⊙▶‖"键，随时播放、暂停语音服务；

如需中英文声音切换，请按"Language"键；

如需调节声音大小，请按"音量+/-"；

妙笔长时间使用后，请及时充电。

Direction for Use

Press the button "⊙▶‖" on the aigopen for 3 seconds to switch on/off, then click on the icon "⊙" at lower right corner of the cover, aigopen will take you to appreciate the oriental ancient capital - the miens at all times of Beijing.

Use the aigopen to click on the icon "⊙" of each picture, and listen to the cultural tale back with a beautiful picture.

Press the button "⊙▶‖" short to activate the play/pause mode of the language service at any time.

Please press "Language" button to change between Chinese and English.

Press "Volume +/-" to adjust the volume.

Please recharge the aigopen immediately after long-time use.

Supporting aigopen point-and-click-reading technology.

责任编辑：秦凤京
撰　　文：王　洋
翻　　译：韩清月　鲁安琪
摄　　影：王文波　王慧明　翟东风　姚天新　蒙　紫
　　　　　赵德春　王希宝　胡敦志　付忠庆　刁立声
　　　　　朱　芗　李　佐　陆　岩　孙玉芬　肖　田
　　　　　宋　红　严向群　陈　宇　王宏林　龚威健
　　　　　王　耕　邢光明　秦凤京
设计制版：北京中文天地文化艺术有限公司

图书在版编目（CIP）数据

北京：汉英对照/王洋编文；韩清月，鲁安琪译；王文波等摄.—北京：中国旅游出版社，2008.7
ISBN 978-7-5032-3499-6

Ⅰ.北… Ⅱ.①王…②韩…③鲁…④王… Ⅲ.北京市—概况—摄影集　Ⅳ.K921-64

中国版本图书馆CIP数据核字（2008）第102770号

书　　名：北京
出版发行：中国旅游出版社
地　　址：北京建国门内大街甲9号
邮政编码：100005
印　　刷：北京顺诚彩色印刷有限公司
版　　次：2008年8月第1版
印　　次：2008年8月第1次印刷
开　　本：850毫米×1168毫米　1/24
印　　张：5
印　　数：1—3000册
定　　价：78.00元
ISBN　978-7-5032-3499-6

（版权所有·翻版必究）

CONTENTS 目录

序 FOREWORD	8

北京的心脏 HEART OF BEIJING — 10

天安门 Tian'anmen	10
天安门广场 Tian'anmen Square	13
人民大会堂 Great Hall of the People	14
国家博物馆 National Museum	14
毛主席纪念堂 Chairman Mao's Memorial Hall	15
人民英雄纪念碑 Monument to the People's Heroes	15

皇家宫苑 IMPERIAL PALACES AND GARDENS — 20

故宫博物院 Palace Museum	20
北海公园 Beihai Park	33
景山公园 Jingshan Park	36
天坛公园 Temple of Heaven	39
颐和园 Summer Palace	45
香山公园 Fragrant Hills Park	50
圆明园遗址公园 Yuanmingyuan Ruins Park	53

名胜古迹 PLACES OF HISTORICAL INTEREST — 55

长城 Great Wall	55
明十三陵 Ming Tombs	66
雍和宫 Lama Temple	70
潭柘寺 Tanzhe Temple	72
戒台寺 Jietai Temple	72
法海寺 Fahai Temple	73
云居寺 Yunju Temple	74
孔庙 Confucius Temple	74
古观象台 Ancient Observatory	76
北京猿人遗址 Peking Man Ruins	78
延庆古崖居 Guyaju Ancient Caves	79
明城墙遗址 Ruins of Ming City Wall	80
菖蒲河公园 Changpu River Park	80
天宁寺古塔 Tianning Temple Pagoda	82
五塔寺 Five Pagoda Temple	82

京味文化 BEIJING CULTURE — 84

什刹海景区 Shichahai Lakes	86
胡同 *Hutong*	88
前门大街 Qianmen Street	90
京剧 Peking Opera	92
杂技 Acrobatics	95
民俗曲艺 Folk Arts	96
琉璃厂古文化街 Liulichang Antiques Street	98
北京烤鸭 Beijing Roast Duck	101

现代都市 MODERN METROPOLIS — 103

中关村 Zhongguancun	103
中央电视塔 CCTV Tower	104
王府井 Wangfujing	106
中国科学技术馆 China Science and Technology Museum	108
首都博物馆 Capital Museum	108
中华世纪坛 China Millennium Monument	109
798艺术园区 798 Art District	110
国家大剧院 National Center for the Performing Arts	111
现代城市交通 Urban Traffic	112
首都国际机场 Capital International Airport	114
2008奥运场馆 2008 Olympic Arenas	116

故宮博物院

故宫全景
A panoramic view of the Palace Museum

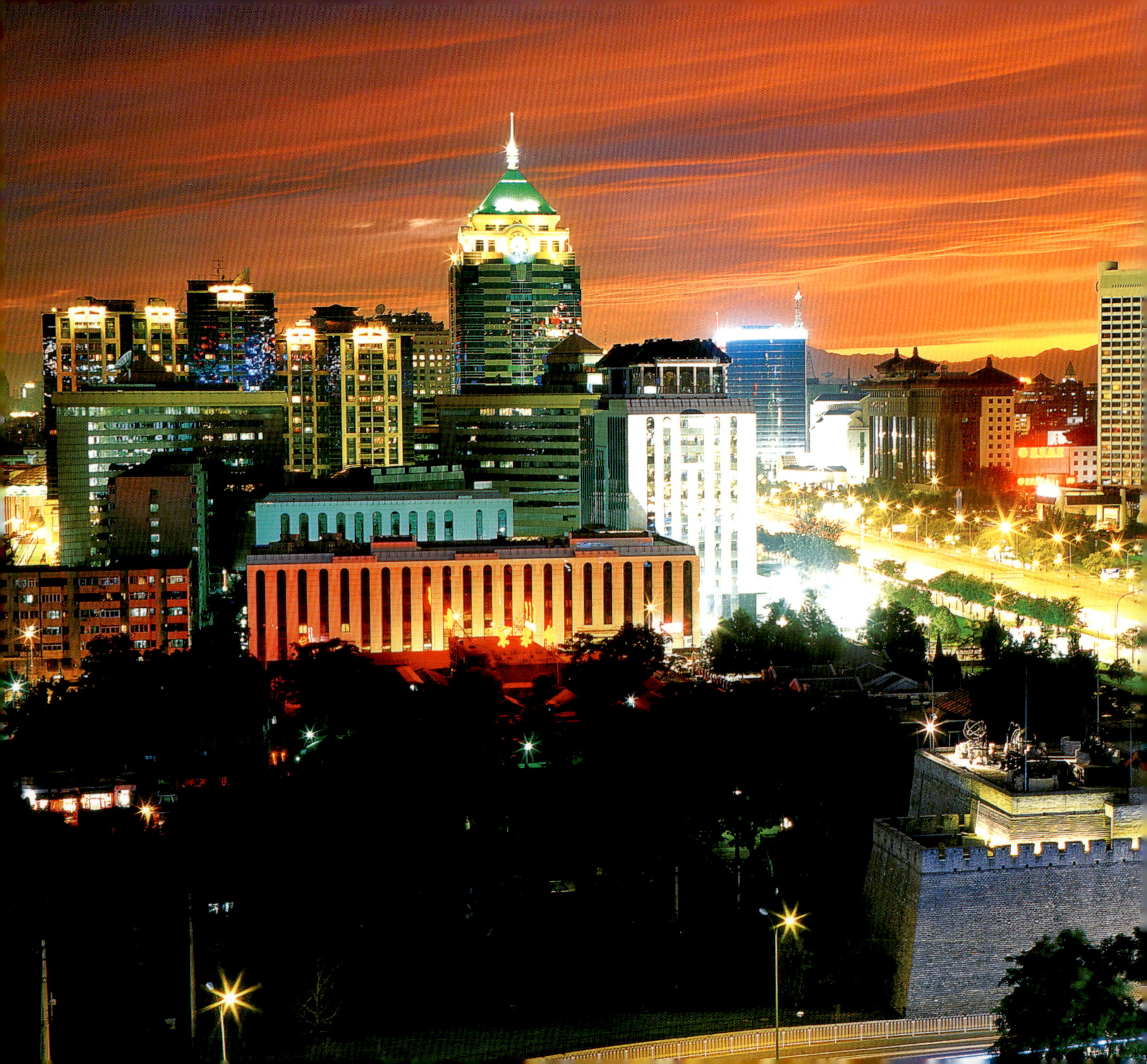

建国门晚霞
Evening glow at Jianguomen

序 Foreword

　　这是一座古老却又洋溢着青春活力的城市。这是一座在不同文化的碰撞下焕发出夺目光彩的城市。

　　北京，中华人民共和国的首都，中国的政治和文化中心，一座在人类文明史册中占有重要位置的城市，世界知名的旅游胜地。

　　北京是一座非凡的城市，她气势恢弘又具有独特的个性。无论是徜徉在有八百余年历史的皇宫林苑，还是漫步在灰墙黛瓦的古老街巷，或是伫立在高楼林立的现代化街区，都会有一种惊奇、一份感叹油然涌上您的心头：深厚的文化底蕴和强烈的现代气息怎么会如此融洽地在这个古老而又年轻的城市中并存着?！

　　这就是北京的魅力。

　　北京很古老。50 万年前，北京出现了会用火、有语言、能够直立行走的北京猿人。他们是世界上最早懂得使用火的原始人类之一。

　　作为一个历史悠久的城市，北京与世界上任何古城相比都毫不逊色。她建城已有 3000 余年，作为都城也有 800 余年的历史。自元世祖忽必烈定都北京开始（1272 年），北京第一次成为中国的政治、经济和文化中心。经过近 10 年的建设，一座以一连串的湖泊衬托着美丽的宫殿和园林，有着规整的棋盘式街道布局的城市诞生了。她就是元大都，是意大利著名旅行家马可·波罗笔下当时世界上最宏伟壮丽的城市。自那以后，她一直是中国最重要的城市和封建王朝的都城。

　　北京很美丽。从 3000 年前一个诸侯国的都邑，到一个有着十几亿人的泱泱大国的首都，数千年各种不同民族文化的融合、数百年帝王之都的熏陶以及百余年东西方文化的碰撞，孕育出成熟大气、凝重醇厚的北京文化。作为中国主流文化中最重要的部分，这种由千年文化积淀陶冶出的、极具地域特色的文化与新世纪的气息交融，形成了奇异而微妙的文化存在，使古城北京体现出一种独特的文化之美。正是这种文化之美，使北京具有了永远的魅力。

　　数百年来，几代王朝的不断建设，为北京留下了无法计数的名胜古迹和文化艺术珍品，使北京成为拥有世界遗产最多的中国城市。人类建筑史上的奇迹万里长城，世界上现存规模最大的皇家建筑群故宫，如诗如画的皇家园林颐和园和北海，世界上最大的祭祀性建筑群天坛，规模宏大的皇家墓寝明十三陵，远古北京人的居所周口店猿人洞，埋藏着千年石刻佛经的房山云居寺，等等，还有香山、潭柘寺、戒台寺等众多设计精妙的公园和寺庙，北京的名胜古迹多得不胜枚举。而那些呈棋盘状构成北京城基本骨架的上千条胡同，以及有着独特韵味的京味文化，更使北京因融合了古城神韵、皇都气度和多层面的市井文化而具有独树一帜的美丽。

　　北京又很现代。作为全国的政治、文化中心，北京城市规模不断扩大，人口不断增加，经济实力不断增强。特别是 20 世纪 80 年代以来，北京以海纳百川的胸怀吸引着国内外、海内外的各类人才和投资。北京是全中国吸引外资最多、人才最集中、信息最发达、现代化程度最高的城市。而 2008 年在北京举办的第 29 届奥运会，更使北京的城市建设和文化建设日新月异，向着国际化的现代都市大步迈进。

　　到过北京的人，无不惊叹她的独特和大气；而长住在北京的人，却会陶醉在她的深邃和丰富之中。

Foreword

Beijing, capital of the People's Republic of China, is the center of the political and cultural life of the country.

An old city full of vigor, it is where different cultures integrate. A well-known tourist destination, it enjoys an important position in the history of human civilization.

Walking in centuries-old royal palaces and gardens, or strolling on the ancient roads and lanes between gray walls and black tiles, or standing in the forest of modern high-rises and skyscrapers, one cannot help wondering how an ancient cultural tradition can be so well maintained in a city imbued with modern breath. This is where the charm of the city lies.

Beijing is an old city. Its history dates back to 500,000 years ago when Peking Man came on stage. Peking Man was one of the earlier human ancestors. They had language, were able to walk fully erect, and knew how to use fire.

Beijing's history as a city lasts over 3,000 years. For more than 800 years, Beijing has served as a capital. It became China's political, economic and cultural center for the first time in history in 1272 when Kublai Khan, the second emperor of the Yuan Dynasty (1206-1368), chose Beijing as his capital. A beautiful and regular city crisscrossed with streets and rivers and dotted with lakes, palaces and gardens was gradually formed in the following two decades. Called Dadu (Grand Capital) then, it was described by Marco Polo as the most prosperous and glorious city in the world of the time.

During its expansion from a small town 3,000 years ago to the capital of a big country with 1.3 billion people, a great and profound culture was formed. Influences from cultures of different ethnicities, feudal dynasties, and sometimes East-West conflicts, can be found in the culture, a unique culture that features a long history, strong local characteristics and fresh air of the new century. This is where Beijing's enduring charm lies.

Beijing is a beautiful city. The expansion and construction since the Yuan Dynasty has continued for centuries, and left behind numerous places of historical interest and cultural relics. Beijing excels other Chinese cities to have the most world heritage sites: Great Wall, a man-made wonder; Palace Museum, the largest imperial complex still exists today; Summer Palace and Beihai Park, the picturesque royal gardens; Temple of Heaven, the world's largest complex for worship heaven; Ming Tombs, the large-size royal burial ground; and Ape Man Cave in Zhoukoudian, a site of primitive residents. It has more to show: Yunju Temple at Fangshan, where thousand-year-old stone carvings of Buddhist sutra can be found; Fragrant Hills, Tanzhe and Jietai temples to name a few.

Beijing is also a modern city. As the national capital of China, Beijing sees its urban scale expanding and its population and economic strength rising. Since the 1980's, the city has opened its door to talents and investment from all over the world, and now leads the country in both aspects. It has built a well-developed information network to become the most modern city in China. The 2008 Olympic Games is bound to promote Beijing's urban and cultural construction and accelerate its pace toward an international metropolis.

No one will leave Beijing without being impressed by its magnificence and unique charm, while the locals feel grateful for the rich and dense cultural environment.

北京的心脏
HEART OF BEIJING

对中国人来说，也许没有一个地方像天安门广场那样令人魂牵梦萦：她是百余年来中华民族许多重大历史事件的见证，她是自信、自立的中华人民共和国的象征，她是北京的心脏。

To the Chinese, no place in China is as important as Tian'anmen Square. For centuries, the square has witnessed numerous historic events. It is the heart of Beijing and a symbol of confidence and self-reliance of the People's Republic.

天安门
Tian'anmen

坐落在天安门广场北端的天安门始建于明永乐十五年（1417年），是昔日的皇宫——紫禁城的正门。明清两朝，它最大的用途是国家有重大庆典，如皇帝登基、册立皇后时在此举行"颁诏"仪式。1949年10月1日，毛泽东主席在天安门城楼上庄严宣布中华人民共和国成立。

Built in 1417 in the Ming Dynasty, the Tian'anmen Rostrum at the north end of the square, was formally the entrance to the Forbidden City. It was where imperial decrees were issued when the emperor ascended the throne or he crowned his empress. It was on this rostrum that late Chairman Mao Zedong announced to the world the founding of the People's Republic of China on October 1, 1949.

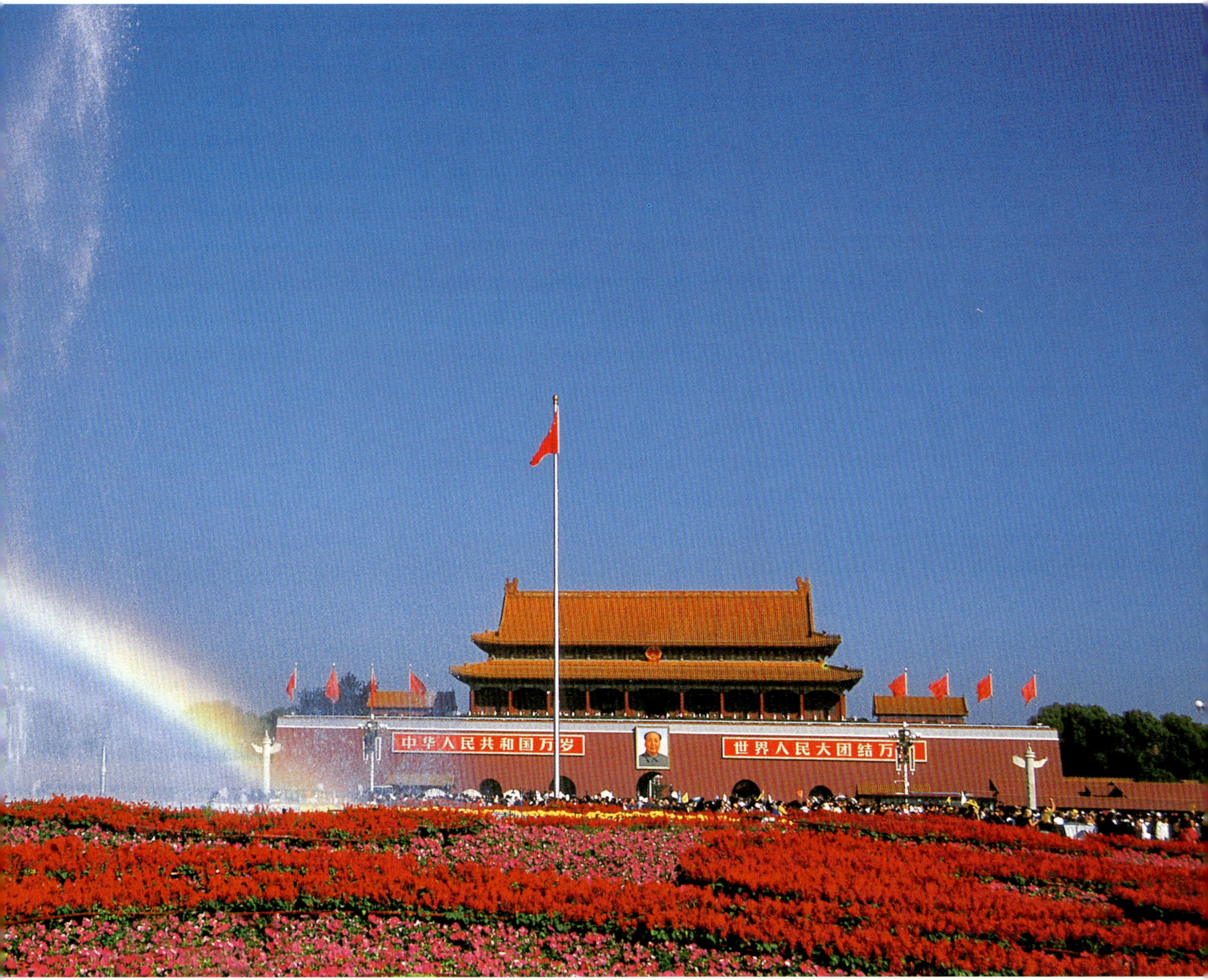
中华人民共和国万岁
世界人民大团结万

升旗仪式
National Flag Raising Ceremony

　　中华人民共和国的国旗——五星红旗在天安门广场上空高高飘扬。每天黎明和黄昏，许多人会肃立在五星红旗周围，等待庄严的升、降国旗仪式。
　　The Five-Star Red Flag, the national flag of the People's Republic of China, is flying high over the square. The daily flag raising ceremony at sunrise and the flag lowering at sunset always attract a large audience.

天安门广场
Tian'anmen Square

　　天安门广场南北长 880 米，东西宽 500 米，总面积达 44 万平方米，可容纳 100 万人举行盛大集会，是世界最大的广场。天安门广场的东侧是中国国家博物馆，西侧是人民大会堂；广场中央高高矗立的人民英雄纪念碑记录着百余年来中国人民民族解放的艰苦历程。纪念碑南侧的毛主席纪念堂于 1977 年落成。每天，有成千上万来自全国和世界各地的人们到天安门广场参观、游览。

The Tian'anmen Square is the largest of its kind in the world. It is 880 meters long from north to south, and 500 meters wide from east to west. Occupying an area of 440,000 square meters, it can accommodate up to one million people at a time. It has the National Museum of China (Chinese Revolutionary Museum and the Chinese History Museum) to the east, and the Great Hall of the People to the west. In the center is the Monument to the People's Heroes, which records the Chinese people's hard struggle for national liberation. To the south of the monument is Chairman Mao's Memorial Hall built in 1977.

人民大会堂
Great Hall of the People

人民大会堂建成于 1959 年，总面积 172 万平方米，是全国人民代表大会常务委员会的办公地点。这座由中央大厅、万人大会堂、7000 平方米的大宴会厅，以及以包括港澳台在内的全国各省、自治区、直辖市的名称命名的厅堂组成的宏大建筑群，当年建设只用了令人难以置信的 10 个月的时间。

The Great Hall of the People, built in 1959 and occupying an area of 1.72 million square meters, is the seat of the Standing Committee of the National People's Congress, China's parliament. It is a great architectural complex consisting of the Central Hall, Ten-Thousand-People Conference Hall, a 7,000-square-meter banquet hall and halls named after provinces, autonomous regions and municipalities directly under the jurisdiction of the Central Government. The construction was finished in 10 months.

中国国家博物馆
National Museum

落成于 1959 年的中国国家博物馆是一座全面、系统地展示中华民族悠久历史与文化，并向中国观众介绍世界优秀文化的综合性博物馆，现有 60 余万件藏品。2007 年 3 月 17 日，中国国家博物馆开始改扩建，扩建后的新馆建筑面积达到 19.2 万平方米，将于 2010 年对观众开放。

A combination of two museums completed in 1959, the National Museum has more than 600,000 collections, displaying China's 5,000 years of civilization. It was renovated starting March 2007 and is scheduled to reopen by 2010 with a 192,000-square-meter floor area.

毛主席纪念堂
Chairman Mao's Memorial Hall

毛主席纪念堂于1979年开放，每天都有许许多多的人满怀崇敬之心前往瞻仰一代伟人的遗容。

Chairman Mao Zedong Memorial Hall was open in 1979. Everyday, many people will come to pay homage to this great man.

人民英雄纪念碑
Monument to the People's Heroes

为纪念自1840年至1949年百余年间为了中华民族的解放而牺牲的先烈，1958年，在天安门广场的中央，建造起碑高37.94米，碑基3000余平方米的人民英雄纪念碑。碑的正面是毛主席题写的"人民英雄永垂不朽"8个镏金大字，背面是周恩来总理题写的碑文，碑座上的8幅大型汉白玉浮雕概括了中国百余年来重要的历史事件。

The Monument to the People's Heroes was set up in 1958 to commemorate martyrs dead for national liberation during 1840-1949. On the front are late Chairman Mao's writing" The people's heroes are immortal!" and on the back is the inscription by late Premier Zhou Enlai. The eight white-marble bas-relief depict the historic events in China during that time.

天安门广场鸟瞰
A bird's-eye-view of the Tian'anmen Square

节日的天安门广场花团锦簇
Tian'anmen Square, a sea of flowers on festivals

中华人民共和国万岁　世界人民大团结万岁

节日之夜，天安门广场礼花绽放
Fireworks over the Tian'anmen Square

皇家宫苑
IMPERIAL PALACES AND GARDENS

金碧辉煌的皇家宫殿群、优美典雅的皇家园林以及延续千年而不断的文化底蕴是北京的骄傲。从世界各地来到北京的旅游者无不希望目睹那些世界闻名的历史遗存。

Magnificent imperial palaces, graceful royal gardens and a thousand-year-old culture are the pride of Beijing and what visitors from around the world are eager to explore.

故宫博物院
Palace Museum

故宫曾被称作紫禁城,是明清两个朝代(1368–1911年)的皇宫,始建于明永乐四年(1406年),历15年建成。故宫东西宽750米,南北长960米,总面积为72万平方米,有房屋近万间,是世界上现存规模最大、保存最完好的皇宫,其建筑风格集中体现了中国建筑的传统和特点,是中国古代建筑的杰作。故宫内藏有明清两个朝代的上千万件档案、书籍和上百万件珍宝、艺术品,其中有许多孤品,是中国最大的博物馆和珍宝馆。1925年,故宫改为博物院,对公众开放;1987年,被联合国教科文组织列入《世界遗产名录》。

The Palace Museum, also known as the Forbidden City, was the imperial palace of the Ming and Qing dynasties (1368-1911). It is 960 meters long from north to south and 750 meters wide from east to south. It is the largest and best-preserved imperial palace in the world, with approximately 10,000 rooms in the 720,000-square-meter compound. It is a masterpiece of traditional Chinese architecture. The Palace Museum, the largest treasure house in China, houses some 10 million books and archives of the Ming and Qing dynasties (many are the only copies), and some 1 million cultural relics and art works. It was turned into a museum and opened to the public in 1925. It was listed as a world cultural heritage site in 1987.

故宫午门与金水桥
The Meridian Gate and the Golden River Bridge

太和殿广场庄严、宏大，体现出皇家的威严。
The grand Hall of Supreme Harmony.

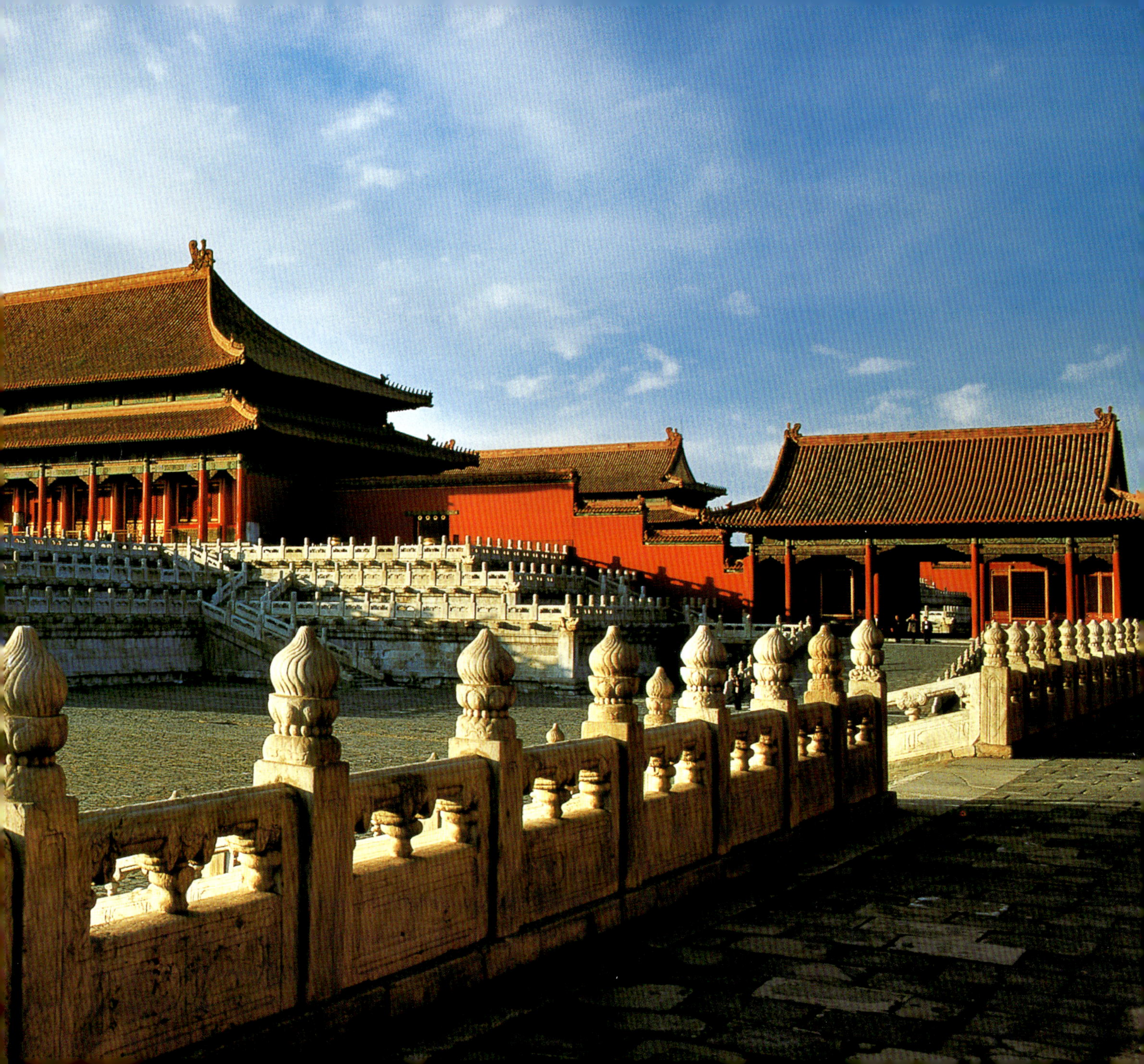

故宫分为两大部分,即外朝和内廷。外朝主体建筑有"三大殿":太和殿、中和殿、保和殿以及侧殿:文华殿和武英殿。"三大殿"是皇帝举行盛大典礼、行使权力及与群臣共议国是的主要场所。

中和殿(前)与保和殿(后)

The Palace Museum can be divided into outer court and inner court. The outer court consists of the Hall of Supreme Harmony, the Hall of Complete Harmony, the Hall of Preserving Harmony and two wing halls of Wenhua and Wuying. The three main halls were where emperors held grand ceremonies, exerted power and discussed national affairs with the ministers.

The Hall of Complete Harmony (front) and the Hall of Preserving Harmony (back)

太和殿俗称金銮殿，是明清皇帝举行重要典礼的场所，在"三大殿"中规模最大，规格最高。

大殿中设雕龙镂空金漆宝座，殿内梁、枋全部沥粉贴金。靠近宝座的六根沥粉蟠龙金柱与宝座上方的金漆蟠龙吊珠藻井，更是充分显示出皇帝的赫赫威仪。

The Hall of Supreme Harmony, the throne hall, was where the Ming and Qing emperors held important ceremonies. It was of the supreme level among all architectures.

In the center of the hall is a gilded throne carved with dragon designs. Also gilded are all the beams and pillars in the hall. The six huge dragon-coiling pillars surrounding the throne and the ceiling with dragon design also signify the supreme power of the emperor.

内廷包括乾清宫、交泰殿、坤宁宫、御花园以及东六宫和西六宫。这里是皇帝处理日常政务以及和嫔妃们居住的地方。乾清宫内的"正大光明"匾是清代自雍正皇帝确立秘密建储制度后，皇帝存放建储密诏的地方。

The inner court consists of the Palace of Heavenly Purity, the Hall of Union and Peace, the Palace of Earthly Tranquility, the Imperial Garden, six east palaces and six west palaces. This was where the emperor managed daily affairs and his concubines lived. The plaque reading" be aboveboard" in the Palace of Heavenly Purity was where some Qing emperors hid away the edict to ordain the crown prince.

乾清宫门外威武的金狮
Golden lion on guard at the Hall of Heavenly Purity

养心殿位于故宫西路，是雍正以后皇帝的寝宫和处理政务的地方。
The Hall of Mental Cultivation was where emperors slept and handled national affairs.

精美华贵的清代"皇后之宝"证明着皇后的地位和身份
The seal of the empress represented her status and dignity

坤宁宫东暖阁，皇帝大婚的洞房。
The east chamber in the Palace of Earthly Tranquility served as the bridal chamber of emperors.

乾隆皇帝朝服像
Emperor QianLong

储秀宫是故宫西六宫之一，慈禧太后晚年曾在这里居住。
The Beauty Accumulating Palace, one of the six west palaces, was where Empress Dowager Cixi lived in her late years.

养心殿东暖阁，慈禧太后在这里垂帘听政。
The east chamber in the Hall of Mental Cultivation, where Empress Dowager Cixi held court from behind a screen.

长春宫寝宫，慈禧曾居此宫。
The Hall of Everlasting Spring, another residence of her.

慈禧太后画像
Empress Dowager Cixi

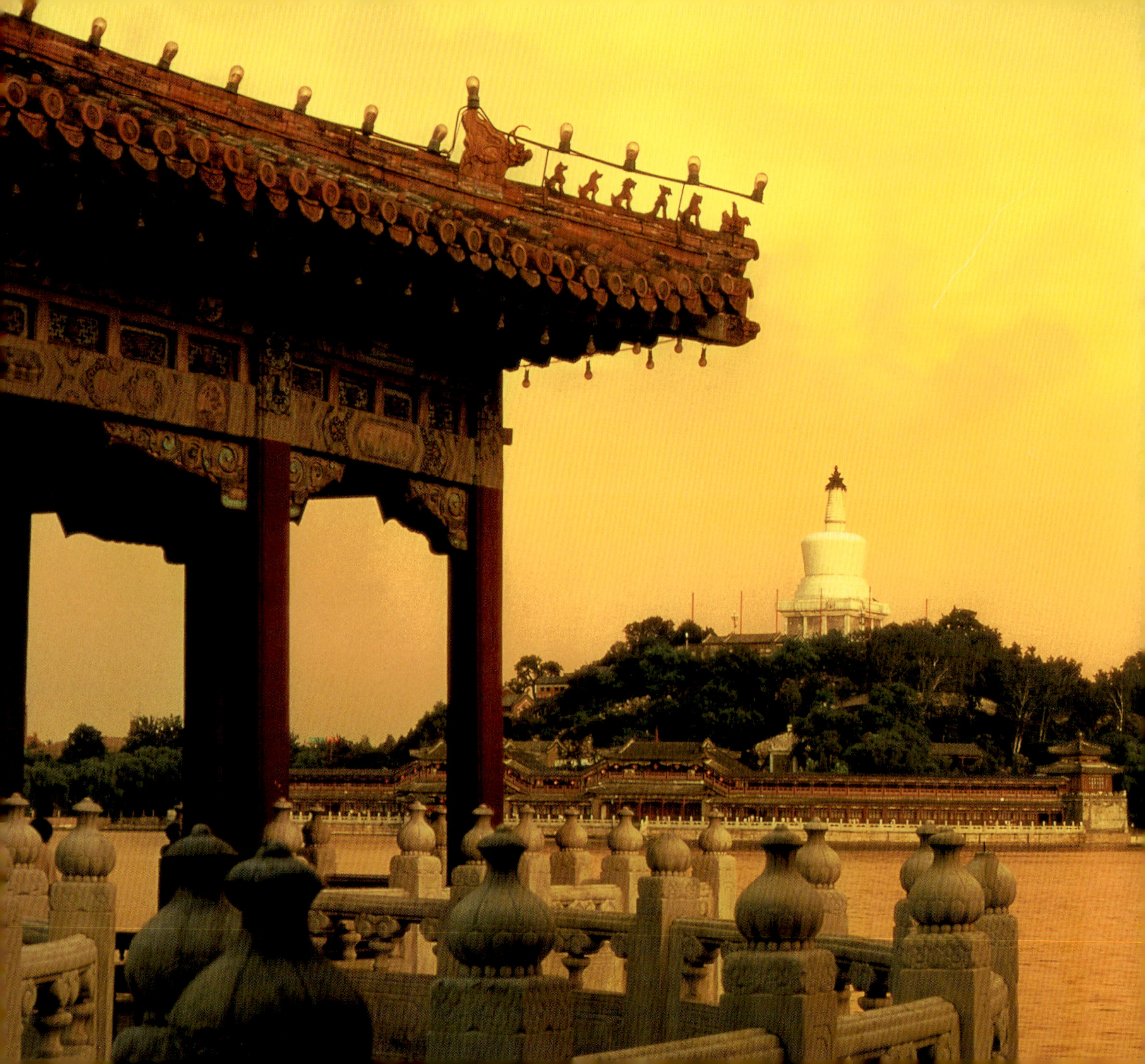

北海公园
Beihai Park

北海是800年前的金朝皇帝按照中国民间"海上仙山"的传说兴建的，历经金、元、明、清几代王朝的建设。北海的面积只有68.2万平方米，但其对于中国园林"移地缩天"原理的运用却是淋漓尽致。这个建筑精巧、布局紧凑、湖光山色的皇家园林有着世界上面积最小的城——团城、五彩斑斓的琉璃影壁——九龙壁、被誉为"海上蓬莱"的琼华岛和美丽的白塔，以及蜿蜒于碧波之上的五龙亭和小巧玲珑、被称为"园中之园"的静心斋等景区，宛若市井之中的一片净土，令人流连忘返。

Beihai Park was built 800 years ago according to the legendary" mountain of immortals on the sea". In the 6.82-hectare ground, there is the Round City, the smallest city in the world; the Nine Dragon Screen, made of colorful glazed tiles; Jade Islet, reputed as a fairy land on the sea; graceful White Pagoda; lakeside Five Dragon Pavilions and Tranquil Mind Study.

用彩色琉璃制成的九龙壁气势非凡，九条龙鲜明灵动，似要破壁而出，堪称华夏琉璃的经典之作。
The Nine Dragon Screen, a masterpiece of glazed tilesmoment.

静心斋是北海的"园中之园"，以小中见大、玲珑幽静为特色。
The Tranquil Mind Study is a quiet garden within the garden.

团城承光殿内供奉的玉佛高 1.5 米，系用一整块玉雕刻而成，雍容华贵、精美绝伦，是清光绪皇帝年间由僧人从缅甸化缘而来，被安置于此。

The 1.5-meter-high jade Buddha enshrined in the Chengguang Hall in the Round city was carved out of a single piece of jade. It was a tribute to Qing Emperor Guangxu by a monk from Myanmar.

景山公园
Jingshan Park

位于故宫迤北，因此被称作"故宫的后花园"。景山始建于元代，明初叫万岁山，清顺治十二年（1655年）改名景山。东侧山下原有一棵古槐树，明朝最后一位皇帝——崇祯皇帝在李自成农民军攻进紫禁城时，走投无路，在古槐树上吊自尽。古槐树已死，现在的槐树是后人补栽的。景山是北京内城全景的最佳观赏处。傍晚时分在景山最高处的万春亭俯瞰北京，近处，紫禁城金碧辉煌、气势恢弘；远方，高楼大厦鳞次栉比，气象万千。

To the north of the Palace Museum is Jingshan. The garden was first built in the Yuan Dynasty. At the eastern foot of the hill, there was an aged Chinese scholar tree. Emperor Chongzhen of the Ming Dynasty hanged himself by the tree when the rebel peasants broke the Forbidden City. The present tree is a substitute to the original one. Jingshan is the best place to view the grand Forbidden City and the forests of high-rises surrounding it.

明末崇祯皇帝自缢处
Spot where Chongzhen, the last emperor of the ming Dynasty, hanged himself in 1644.

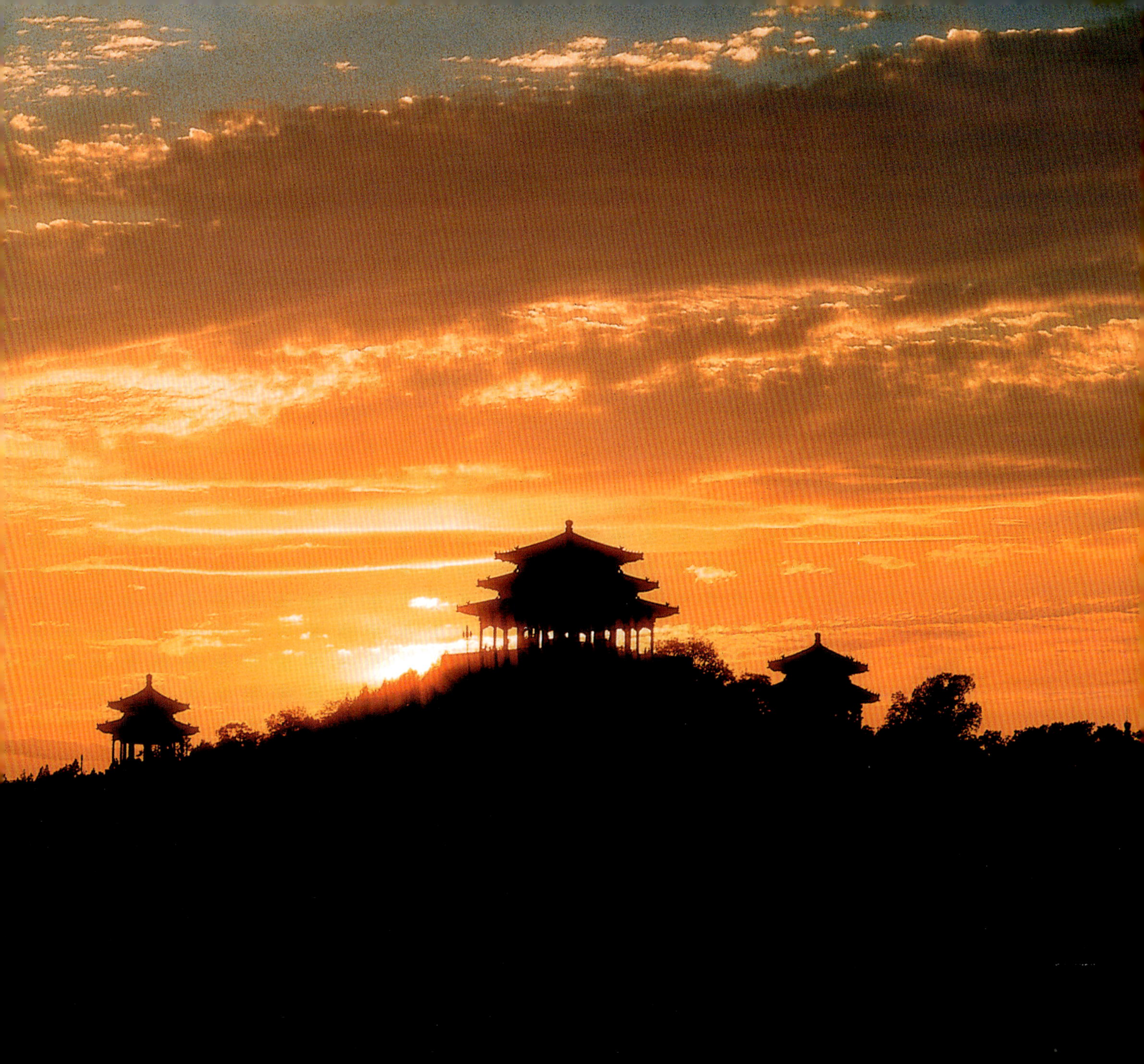

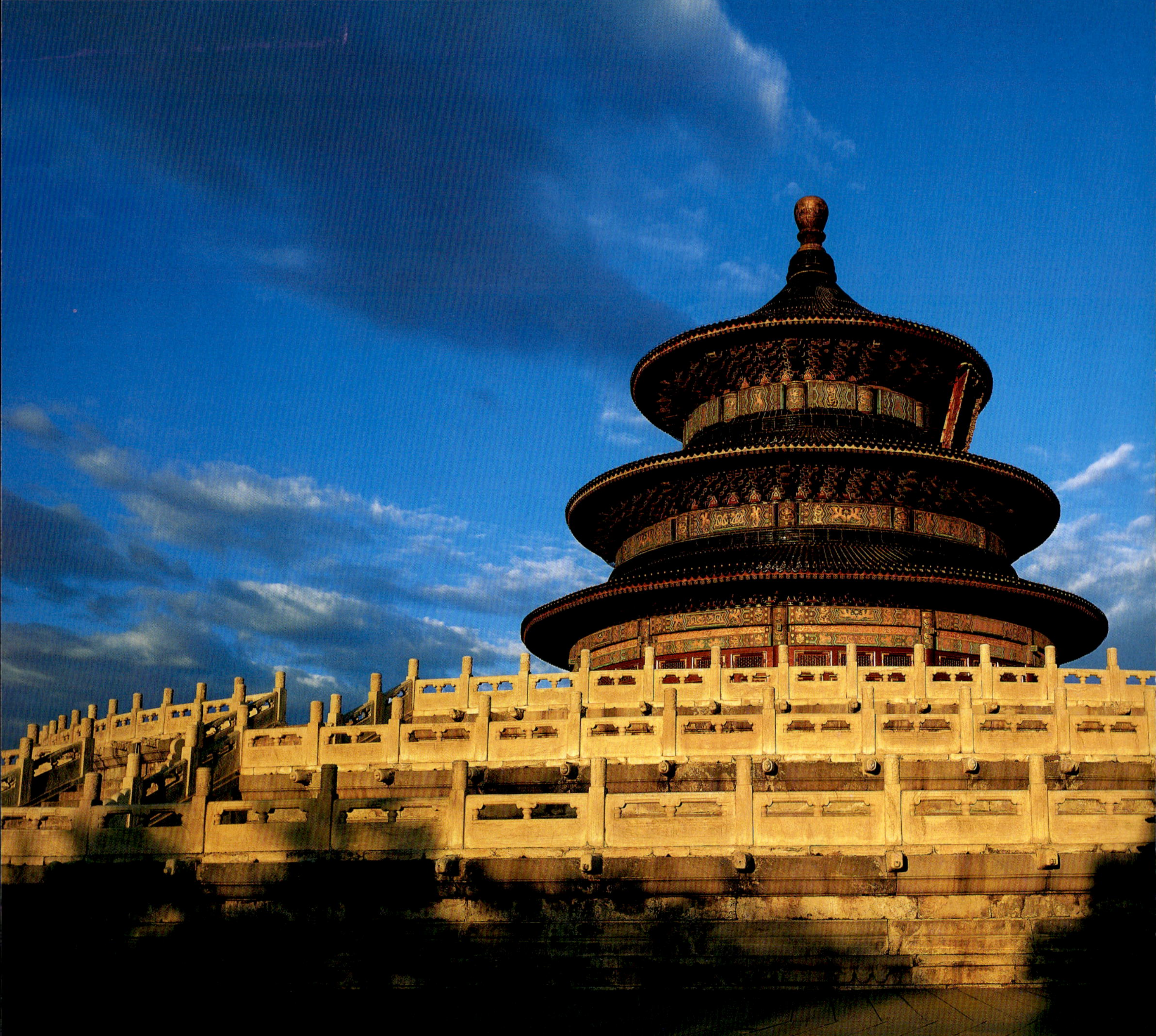

天坛公园
Temple of Heaven

天坛是世界上最大的皇家祭天建筑，始建于明代永乐十八年（1420年），面积273万平方米，是世界上最独特的建筑群之一。她不仅完整地表达了中国人对天、地、神的崇拜，而且体现了古代中国人朴素的宇宙观和高超的建筑艺术。1998年12月，天坛被联合国教科文组织列入《世界遗产名录》。

两道"回"字形的坛墙将天坛分为外坛和内坛，根据中国人"天圆地方"的传统观念，北面的坛墙呈半圆形，象征"天"；南面的坛墙为方形，象征"地"。天坛的主要建筑分布在内坛，北边以祈年殿为中心的一组建筑群叫祈谷坛，皇帝在这里举行祈谷大典，祈求丰年；南面以圜丘、皇穹宇为主的一组建筑群叫圜丘坛，每年冬季，皇帝在这里举行祭天大典。在内坛西侧，还有一组建筑是斋宫，举行祭天仪式前，皇帝先要在斋宫戒斋、沐浴，以示虔诚。

明清两朝，作为皇家的祭天场所，天坛广植松柏。今天，随处可见的百年松柏与庄严神秘的祭坛一起营造出一种古朴典雅、祥和宁静的氛围，使天坛更具魅力。

Built in 1420 and occupying an area of 27.3 hectares, the Temple of Heaven is the world's largest imperial architecture for worshiping heaven, and one of the unique architectural complexes in the world. It not only expresses the adoration of the ancient Chinese towards the heaven, the earth and the divinities, but also reflects their simple concept about the universe and superb architecture. The Temple of Heaven was listed on the UNESCO World Heritage list in December 1998.

The extire complex is surrounded by two layers of walls. According to traditional Chinese concept of" circular heaven and square earth", the wall in the north is circular, symbolizing the heaven, while the wall in the south is square, implying the earth. In the north of the complex is the Hall of Prayer for Good Harvest, a magnificent piece mounted on a three-tiered marble terrace. It was where the emperors held grand ceremonies to pray for good harvests. In the south of the complex are the Round Altar and the Imperial Vault of Heaven, where the emperors held sacrificial rites. In the west is the Hall of Abstinence, where the emperors prepared themselves for the solemn occasion by spending a night fasting.

As an imperial sacrificial ground in the Ming and Qing dynasties, pines and cypress were densely planted. Today, people can still feel the solemn and quite atmosphere created by the mystic buildings and old trees.

祈年殿是一座无与伦比的建筑。这座高38米、直径32.72米的圆形建筑仅凭木榫交接，斗拱支架，不用一根铁钉，就完成了奇妙的架构，是中国木结构建筑的登峰造极之作。殿内的4根楠木大柱象征四季，12根朱漆金柱代表了12个月，体现了中国古代对于天文历法的精确计算与研究水平。

The Hall of Prayer for Good Harvests is not only splendid in outer appearance, but also unique in inner frame. The 38-meter-hight circular structure, with a diameter of 32.72 meters, is supported entirely by wooden pillars, bars, laths, joints and rafters. Not a single iron nail was used. The four central nanmu pillars represent the four seasons, the twelve pillars in the inner ring symbolize the twelve months, and another 12 in the outer ring the twelve divisions of the day and night.

皇穹宇是存放神位的地方。这座被蓝琉璃瓦覆盖的圆形建筑高 19.5 米，直径 15.6 米。

The Imperial Vault of Heaven was used to contain tablets of the emperor's ancestors. It is a circular building, 19.5 meters high and 15.6 meters in diameter, covered with blue glazed tiles.

皇穹宇最奇妙的部分是回音壁：站在皇穹宇围墙边小声说话，相隔十余米，站在围墙另一边的人能够清晰地听到。这说明，500 年前的中国人已经能够将声学原理运用于建筑之中。

The most wonderful part is the Echo Wall, which enables a whisper to travel clearly from one end to the other. This indicates that the Chinese had already learned to apply the acoustic theory into buildings as early as 500 years ago.

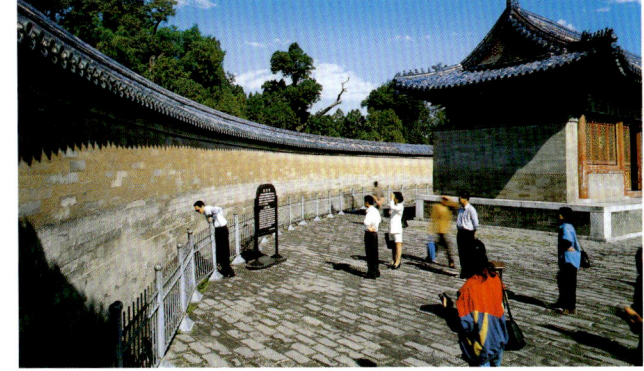

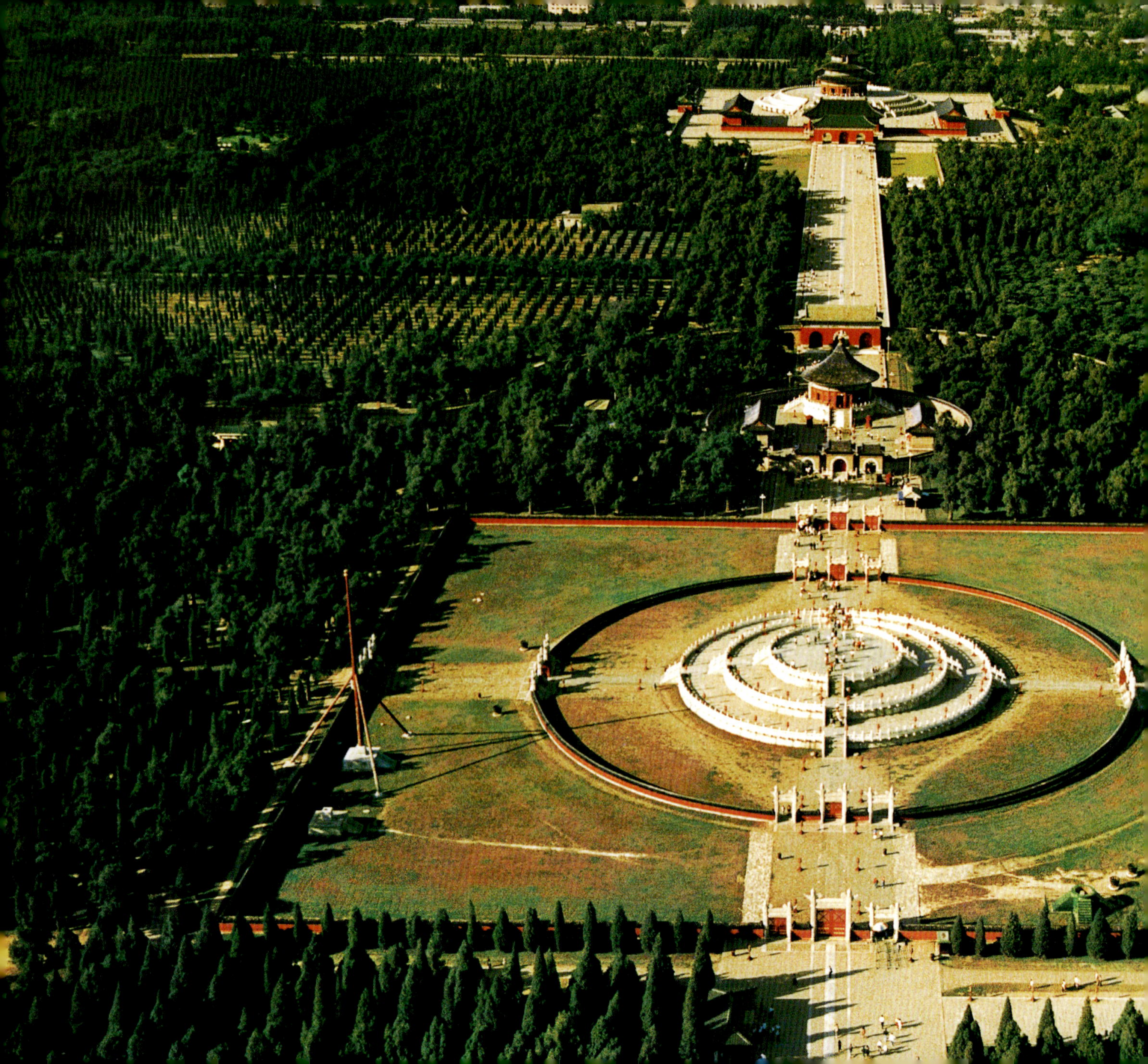

圜丘坛棂星门
The Lingxing Gate to the Circular Mound Altar

斋宫的正殿——无梁殿
The beamless hall in the Hall of Abstinence

　　圜丘坛是一座三层的汉白玉圆坛，建于1530年，高5.17米，最上层直径23.65米。坛中央是一块圆石，称为"天心石"，被9圈扇形石板围绕。从最内圈的9块开始，以9的倍数向外扩展，象征"天"数。

　　The Circular Mound Altar is 5.17 meters high and 23.65 meters in diameter on the top. At the center of the altar lies a round stone surrounded by nine concentric rings of stones. The number of stones in the innermost ring is nine, in the second ring 18 and so on, up to the 81 in the ninth ring.

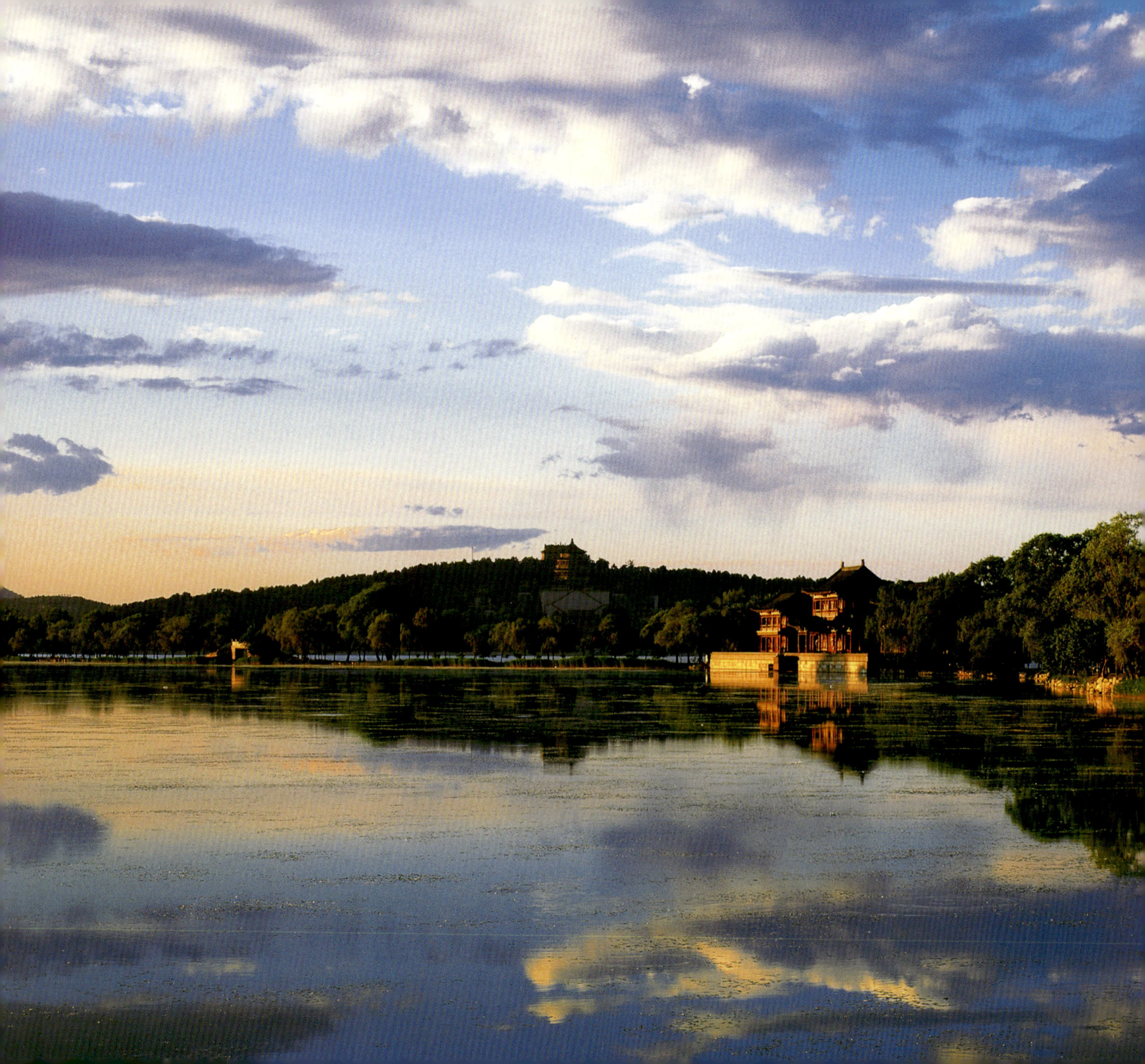

颐和园
Summer Palace

颐和园是清朝皇家园林，总面积达290万平方米。颐和园始建于清乾隆十五年（1750年），原名清漪园。1860年被英法联军焚毁。光绪十二年（1886年），慈禧太后挪用海军经费重修，并改名为颐和园。1998年颐和园被联合国教科文组织列入《世界遗产名录》。

颐和园又被称为"夏宫"，是清朝皇帝夏季避暑和处理政务的地方。她巧借自然山水修建，主体景观以宏伟的万寿山佛香阁为中心递次铺开，依山就势，错落有致，美丽壮观。面积达220万平方米的昆明湖为这座世界名园平添了灵秀之气。从湖上眺望万寿山、佛香阁，湖光山色犹如一幅立体画卷，令人陶醉。颐和园浓缩了北方园林的壮美和南方园林的绮丽，既有人工妙算，却又浑然天成，集中了中国园林建筑的精华，堪称中国园林的博物馆。

The original Summer Palace was laid out in 1750, and was burnt down by the British and French allied forces during the second Opium War (1860). Empress Dowager Cixi had it rebuilt in 1886 with funds for navy development.

Covering 29 hectares, this was the summer retreat of the imperial households. Most of it is taken up by the 22-hectare Kunming Lake. The panoramic view from the top of the Longevity Hill, the focal point of the Summer Palace, is well worth the climb. The picturesque place blends the cream of gardens in both north and south China. It can be said a museum of Chinese gardens.

颐和园春色旖旎
Spring in the Summer Palace

佛香阁是一座三层八面四重檐的木结构建筑，高41米，是观览颐和园全景的最佳处。

The 41-meter-tall Tower of Buddhist Incense has three stories. It is the best place to overlook the entire complex.

中国民间传说，将铜牛或铁牛放置在河湖之畔可以镇压水患。铸造于1755年的铜牛卧守在昆明湖东岸，好像是在为皇家尽责。铜牛的背上有篆书铭刻的乾隆皇帝御笔《金牛铭》。

As a bronze or iron ox was believed to be able to control the lake flood, so came this bronze one cast in 1755. The inscriptions on its back were handwriting of Qing Emperor Qianlong.

乐寿堂，慈禧太后在颐和园的寝宫。
The Hall of Happiness and Longevity, Empress Dowager Cixi's bedroom in the Summer Palace.

万寿山的后山，温雅秀丽、酷似江南水乡的苏州街和按照佛教意境建造的四大部洲，与山前的宏大华丽形成了鲜明对照。

At the backside of the Longevity Hill, there are Suzhou Street, a model of water town in south China, and Four Great Continents built in Buddhist conception.

玉澜堂，光绪皇帝在颐和园的寝宫。
Hall of Jade Ripples, Emperor Guangxu's bedroom in the Summer Palace.

拥有273间、长达728米、绘有14000幅苏式彩画的长廊，像一条彩练串联起万寿山和东宫门的宫殿区。

The Long Corridor is 728 meters long with 273 sections. The beams of the corridor are painted with more than 14,000 paintings. It likes a silk ribbon connecting the Longevity Hill with the palaces at the East Palace Gate.

香山公园
Fragrant Hills

香山位于北京城的西部，是一处著名的园林风景区，香山公园在清代叫静宜园，是清代著名的皇家园林"三山五园"之一。最高峰海拔557米，因难于攀登被称作"鬼见愁"。香山满山遍植枫树、黄栌，每当秋季来临，层林尽染，万山红遍，游人争相前往观赏。

Located in west Beijing, it is a well-known scenic spot, especially as one of the "three hills and five gardens" for the imperial families in the Qing Dynasty. it is a well-known scenic spot. The highest peak is 557 meters above sea level. In autumn, the frosted maples and smoke trees dye the hills into a yellowish red world.

香山脚下的团城演武厅建于清乾隆十三年（1748年），又称"阅武楼"，建有城池、殿宇、碉楼等，乾隆皇帝当年常在这里阅兵或观看士兵操练。
At the foot of the Fragrant Hills is a Qing Dynasty military structure built in 1748. Emperor Qianlong had watched, from the tower, the soldiers parading or practicing.

每年的金秋时节，香山游人摩肩接踵，绚丽的自然画卷让游人流连忘返。
Autumn sees the most visitors to the Fragrant Hills.

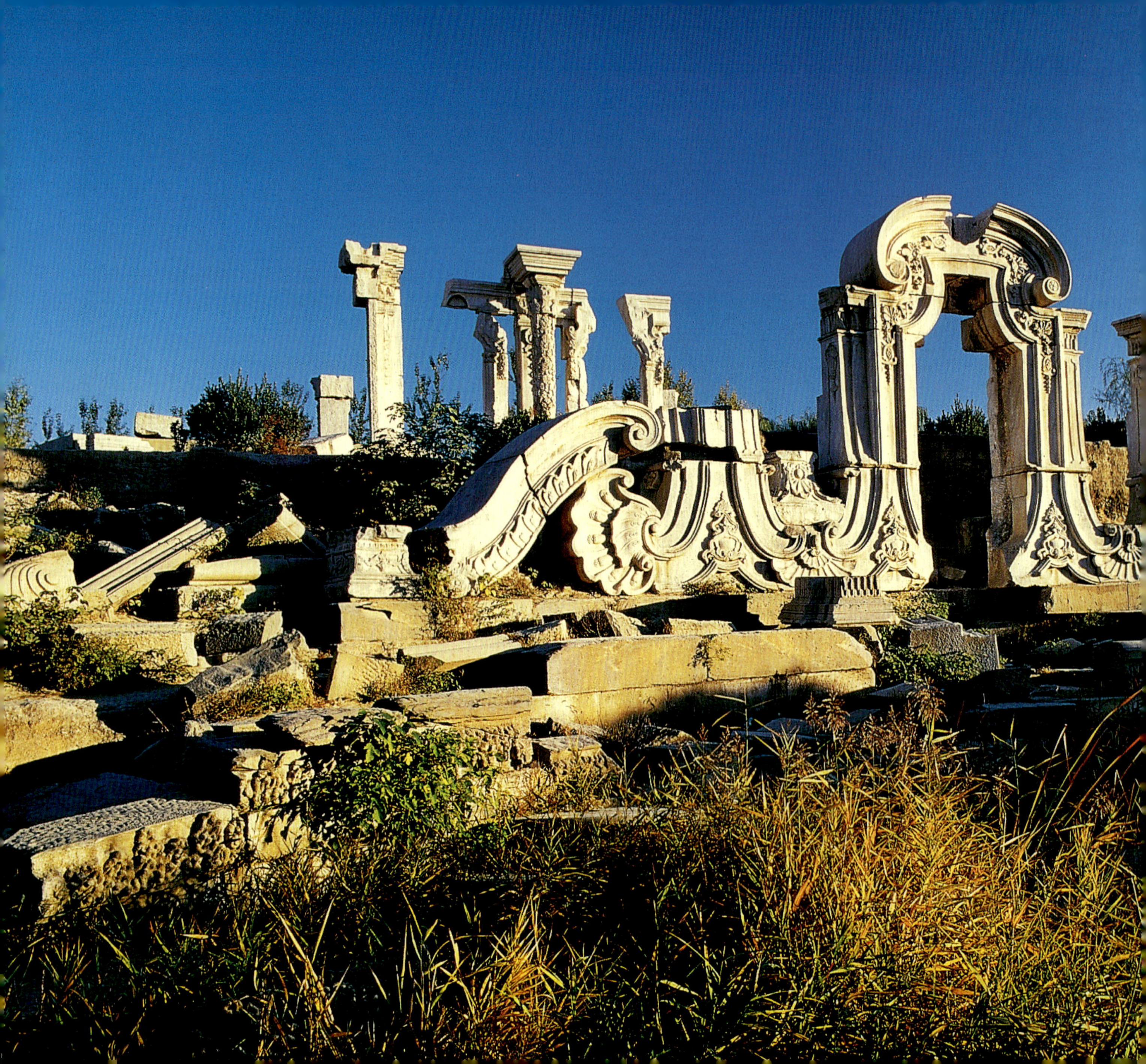

圆明园遗址公园
Yuanmingyuan

　　圆明园位于颐和园东侧，是比颐和园还大的皇家御园，因面积最大、景点最多、最精美而被称为"万园之园"。1860年被入侵北京的英法联军焚毁，1983年开辟成遗址公园。

　　Yuanmingyuan is located to the east of the Summer Palace. It was called " the best of all gardens" for its large scale, wealth of attractions and exquisite workmanship. It was burnt down in 1860 by the British and French allied army. It has opened as a ruin park in 1983.

53

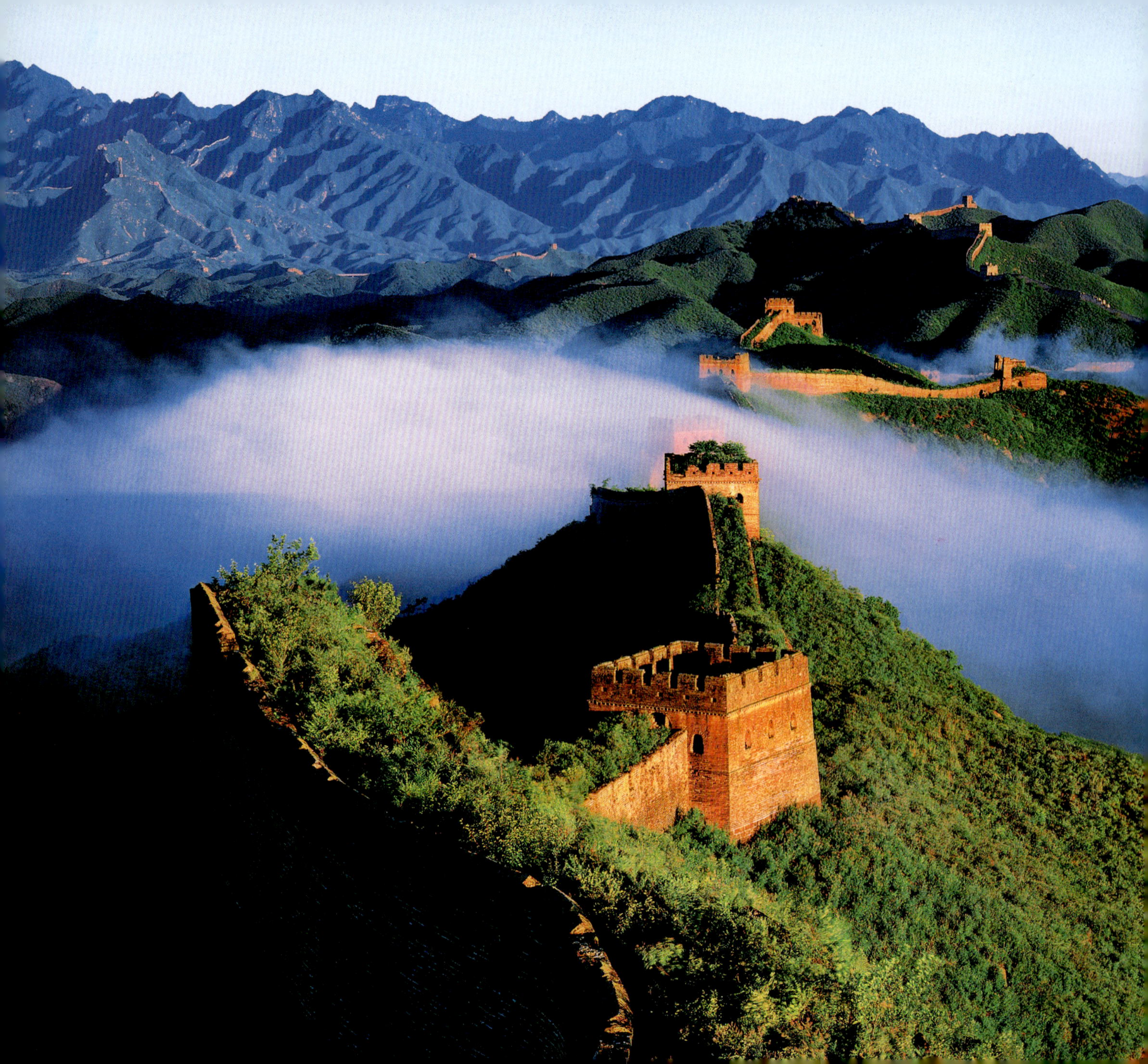

名胜古迹
PLACES OF HISTORICAL INTEREST

无论是旅游者还是长住北京的居民，北京的名胜古迹对他们都具有长久的吸引力。历尽沧桑的古迹成为今天的名胜，像一部浓缩的历史，引人去阅读、去品味。

Places of historical interest have strong attraction toward Beijing residents and tourists alike. These historical monuments just like a condensed history book inviting you to read and explore.

长城
Great Wall

毛泽东诗词中有一句堪称家喻户晓的名句"不到长城非好汉"，这句话现在也成了来中国旅游的外国旅游者人人皆知的名言。被誉为世界建筑史奇迹的万里长城在北京北部山区，绵延 600 余公里，像一座屏障，保护着古代中原不会受到异族的侵扰。这个始建于 2000 余年前的人类最伟大的工程在北京留下了其最壮观、最精华的部分。作为拱卫京师的军事要冲，北京地区的八达岭、慕田峪、司马台长城在永乐年间重修，现在是北京最有吸引力的旅游名胜。1987 年，万里长城被联合国教科文组织列入《世界遗产名录》。

"If we fail to reach the Great Wall we are not men", this line from Mao Zedong's poem now might be known to all, to both Chinese and foreign visitors. The long wall, zigzagging for about 600 kilometers in Beijing's mountainous north, had protected the ancient capital from invasions. The greatest man-made structure on earth, first built 2,000 years ago, has its most wonderful sections in Beijing. As strategic posts, the Badaling, Mutianyu and Simatai sections were reconstructed during the Yongle reign period (1403-1425) of the Ming Dynasty. Now they are the highlights of a Beijing tour. The Great Wall was put on the UNESCO's World Heritage list in 1987.

八达岭长城是长城最著名的地段，位于北京西北郊延庆县关沟北口，是扼守京北的咽喉要道。长城起伏蜿蜒，如苍龙凌空飞舞，雄伟壮观。

Badaling is the best-known section of the Great Wall. Located in Yanqing County, northwest of Beijing, it is of strategic importance in ancient China.

如果说八达岭长城的特色是雄伟，那么，慕田峪长城的特色就是秀丽。慕田峪位于北京东北郊的怀柔区，这一带植被繁茂，春花秋叶、夏荫冬雪，长城四季景色不同，极具观赏价值。

Not as spectacular as Badaling, the Mutianyu section, in northeast Huairou District, looks more elegant with dense vegetation.

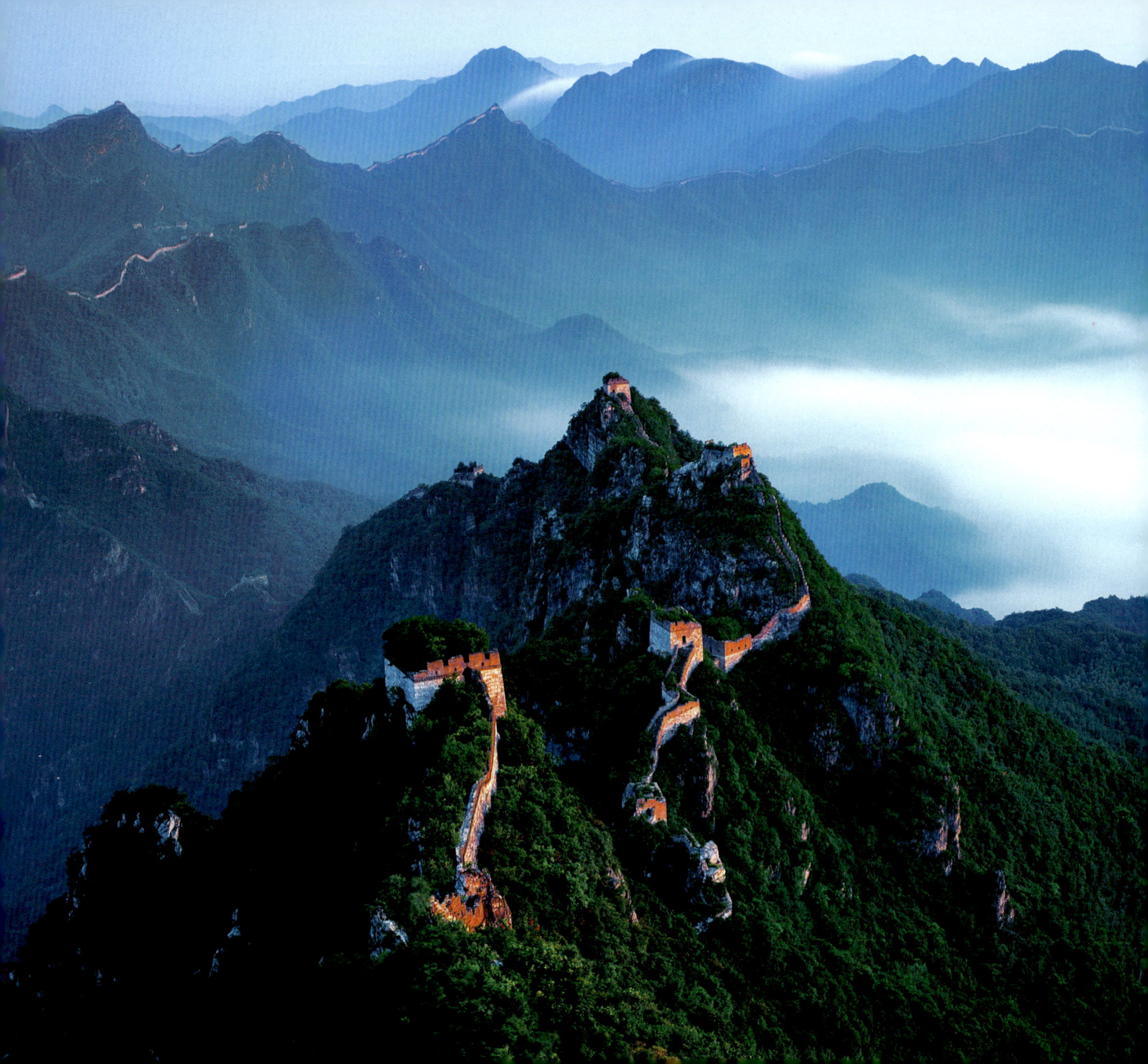

慕田峪长城的建筑很独特，城墙多为双面垛口，敌楼密集，便于防御。特别是箭扣一带，长城往往矗立在绝壁之上，给人"无限风光在险峰"之感。

The Mutianyu section is known for its unusual fortification. Watchtowers are densely built for defensive purpose. The section near Jiankou was built on cliffs.

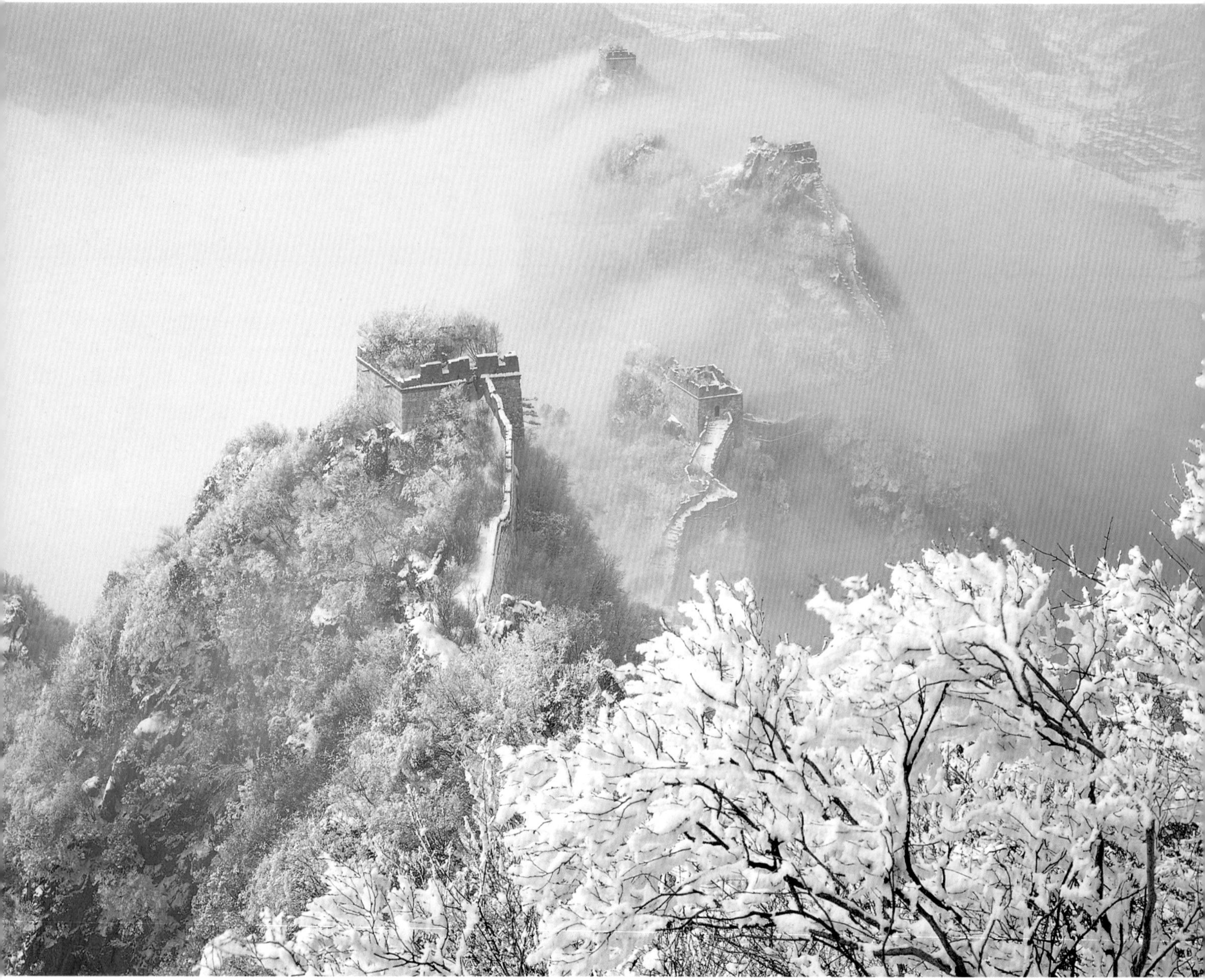

山舞"银龙"（左页图）
A silver "dragon"

雾锁"箭扣"
Jiankou in fog

司马台长城蜿蜒于北京东北郊密云县境内的崇山峻岭之上,以险峻著称。这一带峰峦起伏连绵,长城依山势建在山脊之上,城墙及敌楼的形式变化多端,被专家誉为"中国长城之最"。

The Simatai section winds along the rising and falling steep mountains in Miyun County in northeast Beijing. Simatai is known for diverse parapets and watchtowers.

司马台长城最高海拔为986米,绝壁之上,一座敌楼兀立峰巅。民间传说晴天的夜晚,站在敌楼上可以望见京城的灯火,因而得名望京楼。

The highest point at Simatai is Viewing Beijing Tower built on a cliff 986 meters above sea level. It is said that on the night of a fine day, one can see the lights in Beijing from here.

居庸关是万里长城中最著名的关隘之一,在北京城西北 50 公里处,地势绝险,景色迷人。

The Juyong Pass, one of the major passes on the long wall, is located 50 kilometers northwest of Beijing.

居庸关云台
Cloud Terrace

居庸关保存有元代遗留下来的汉白玉云台，上面精美的元代浮雕和用六种文字撰写的陀罗尼经的经文具有很高的文物价值和艺术欣赏价值。

The Juyong Pass has a well-preserved white-marble terrace of the Yuan Dynasty. On the terrace are exquisite carvings in relief and sutra written in six languages.

明十三陵
Ming Tombs

　从北京城向北行 50 公里，天寿山脚下有一片排列成弧状的金碧辉煌的建筑群，这就是明代皇帝的陵寝十三陵。十三陵埋葬着明朝的 13 位皇帝、23 位皇后，距今已有 500 余年的历史。每座陵墓由祾恩殿、明楼（又称宝顶）和地宫（陵墓）组成。明十三陵中最大的陵是长陵，它是明朝第三位皇帝明成祖朱棣的陵寝，其祾恩殿的规模与故宫的太和殿相仿。现在，明十三陵中只有定陵已被挖掘、开放，游客可以进入地宫，一睹明代皇帝的丧葬方式和被发掘出来的精美文物。

　At the foot of Mt. Tianshuo 50 kilometers north of Beijing, there is a resplendent architectural complex: the Ming Tombs. Here 13 Ming emperors and 23 empresses were buried 500 years ago. Each tomb has a main hall and a tower on the ground, and an underground palace. Changling is the tomb of Zhu Di, the third emperor of the Ming Dynasty. It is the largest of the 13 tombs, and its main hall has a similar scale as the Hall of Supreme Harmony in the Palace Museum. So far, only Dingling has been excavated and opened to tourists.

地宫入口
Entrance to the underground palace

定陵出土的凤冠
Phoenix coronet unearthed from Dingling

定陵埋葬着明万历皇帝朱翊钧和他的两位皇后。地宫面积达1195平方米，为石拱券无梁结构。地宫中出土的3000余件文物，件件精美绝伦，反映了中国的纺织、雕刻、铸造和编织等工艺在明代已达到了非常高的水平。

Dingling buries Emperor Wanli and his two empresses. The 1,195-square-meter underground palace is a beamless stone structure. More than 3,000 cultural relics unearthed show the high technology in textile, carving, casting and weaving in the Ming Dynasty.

明十三陵神路的起点——石牌坊
The stone archway, the starting point of the sacred way in the tomb area

永陵明楼 Yongling

排列在明十三陵神路两旁的 12 尊石人、24 尊石兽雕工精美、线条洗练。
The sacred way is flanked by stone statues, 12 generals and 24 animals. Witnessing different weathers in 500 years, they still look very vivid today.

昭陵祾恩门 Zhaoling

69

雍和宫
Lama Temple

为了巩固多民族的国家,清朝皇帝十分注重与西藏、蒙古的贵族和宗教界的关系。清朝皇帝曾数次接见藏区宗教领袖,并将北京的一座王府——雍和宫改为喇嘛庙。

雍和宫初建于清康熙三十三年(1694年),曾是雍正皇帝继位前的府邸。乾隆九年(1744年),雍和宫正式改为喇嘛庙,成为清政府管理全国喇嘛教事务的中心。

雍和宫有藏传佛教博物馆之称,保存有大量的佛教文物和资料、图片。雍和宫万福阁供奉的木雕弥勒菩萨像由一整根白檀香木雕刻而成,直径3米,高18米,加上埋在地下的8米,共有26米高。传说这根巨大无比的白檀香木来自尼泊尔,七世达赖喇嘛将它运至京城用了三年的时间。

To consolidate the multi-ethnic group country, the Qing emperors attached much importance to the relations with Tibetan and Mongolian nobles and religious personages. They had on several occasions met with the religious leaders, and had a prince's mansion turned into a lamasery.

The Lama Temple was once the residence of Emperor Yongzheng before he succeeded to the throne. In 1744, the complex was made a lamasery and center for the Qing governor to manage national Lamaism affairs.

The temple keeps a large number of Buddhist relics, documents and photos and is called" museum of Tibetan Buddhism". The Mandala Buddha enshrined in Ten-Thousand-Buddha Tower is 26 meters high and three meters in diameters. It was carved out of a single piece of sandal wood and presented by the seventh Dalai Lama. It took three years to transport it to Beijing from Nepal.

每年农历正月二十九至二月初一，雍和宫都要"打鬼"。"打鬼"是喇嘛教的一种宗教仪式，藏语叫做"跳布扎"，即由僧侣装扮成鬼神的模样表演宗教舞蹈。

From the 29th day of the first lunar month to the first day of the second lunar month, the Lama Temple will "beat ghosts", a religious dance performed by monks in disguise of ghosts and divinities.

雍和宫山门
Entrance to the Lama Temple

雍和宫大殿前青铜铸造的须弥山是一件精美的佛教艺术品
The bronze hill before the main hall is an exquisite Buddhist artwork

潭柘寺
Tanzhe Temple

潭柘寺是北京地区历史最悠久的寺庙，最早建于晋代（265～317年），比北京城还要古老。北京古称幽州，因而民间早有"先有潭柘，后有幽州"之说。

Tanzhe Temple came into being in the Jin Dynasty (265~317) before the formation of Beijing city. It is the oldest temple in Beijing.

戒台寺
Jietai Temple

戒台寺距潭柘寺不远，始建于唐武德五年（662年），以全国寺庙最大的戒台和古树、奇松著称。

Not far from Tanzhe Temple is the Jietai Temple. Jietai was built in 662 and is known for its Abstinence Platform, the largest in China, and its ancient trees and pines.

法海寺
Fahai Temple

　　法海寺在北京城西的石景山区，明正统八年（1443年）建成。寺庙坐落于群山环抱之中，环境清幽秀丽，所存文物众多，并存有三棵古柏。

　　Fahai Temple, in Shijingshan District in west Beijing, was built in 1443. The tranquil place nestling in the hills is known for its rich relics and three ancient cypress trees.

　　法海寺大雄宝殿内绘有大型壁画，为明代皇家画师绘于正统八年（1443年）。壁画用沥粉贴金，十分华贵精美，是中国明代壁画的最高典范，亦是不可多得的古代艺术珍宝。

　　The large fresco in the main hall was the work of the Ming royal artists in 1443. It represents the highest level of fresco art in the Ming Dynasty.

云居寺
The Yunju Temple

云居寺位于北京城西南房山区的白云山麓。公元6世纪的隋代,一位名叫静琬的高僧,为使佛经世代留存而发愿刻经。自静琬和尚起,历代有僧人和石匠到云居寺雕刻石经,前后延续了千余年,留下了隋唐辽金元明各朝所刻石经板14620块,因此,云居寺被称作"北京的敦煌",房山石经也被称作"石刻长城"。

Yunju Temple is located at the foot of White Cloud Mountain in Fangshan District in southwest Beijing. In the 6th century, Jingwan, an accomplished monk, began to carve Buddhist scripture on stones as a way to pass them on. In the following 1,000 years, monks and craftsmen continued the work, and left a total of 14,620 pieces of slab stones carved with Buddhist scripture.

云居寺北塔为辽代砖砌舍利塔(上图)
Stupa built in the Liao Dynasty

云居寺东北石经山上凿有9个藏经洞,藏有4196块隋唐时期刻制的石经板,向后人诉说着古代僧侣对信仰的虔诚。为了保护珍贵的文化遗产,1999年9月9日,石经板被妥善回藏到新建的、具有完善保护功能的地宫中。(下图)

On the hill to the northeast of the temple are nine caves that once housed 4,196 stone slabs carved with scriptures in the Sui and Tang dynasties. To better protect them, these precious relics were moved to an underground room in the temple in September 1999.

孔庙
Confucius Temple

孔庙位于东城区的国子监街,始建于元代,清光绪年间重修扩建,是全国第二大孔庙。(右页图)

Confucius Temple on Beijing's Guozijian Street is the second largest, next only to the one in Shandong's Qufu, home of Confucius (551-479 BC), the great thinker and educator. It was first built in the Yuan Dynasty and was renovated and expanded in the 19th century.

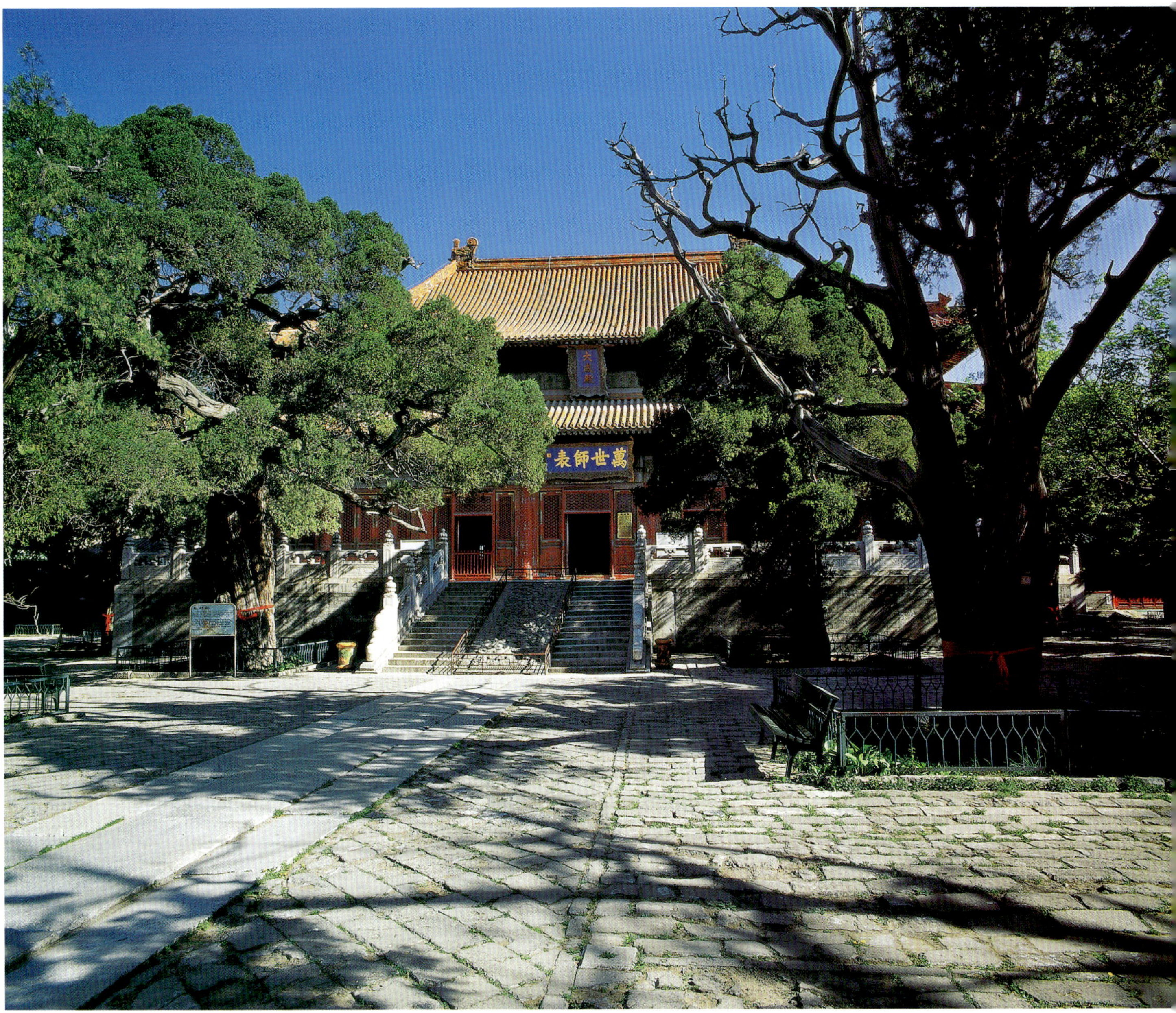
萬世師表

古观象台
Ancient Observatory

北京古观象台是世界著名的观象台之一，建于明正统七年（1442年）。从那时起至1929年，古观象台保持了连续487年的天文观测记录。那些造型精美、铸造精密的大型铜制天文仪器是中国古代天文学的骄傲。

Beijing Ancient Observatory, built in 1442, is one of the well-known observatories in the world. It had kept 487 years of continuous astronomical observations until 1929. The large fine copper equipment is the pride of ancient Chinese astronomy.

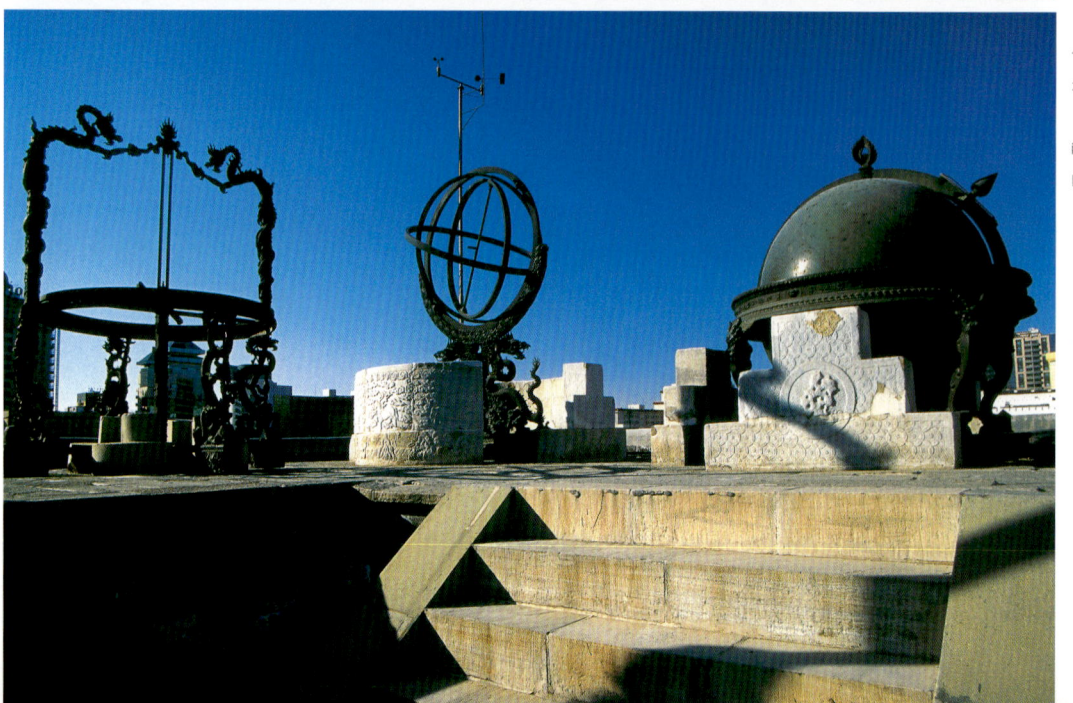

古观象台上陈列着玑衡抚辰仪、天体仪、赤道经纬仪等清代初年制造的大型铜质天文仪器。

Large copper astronomical instrument made in early Qing Dynasty.

赤道经纬仪，制于清代康熙十二年（1673年），主要用于测定真太阳时、天体的赤经差和赤纬。（右页图）

Equatorial Armilla, made in 1673 for the purpose of determining true solar time as well as the right ascension difference and declination of celestial bodies.

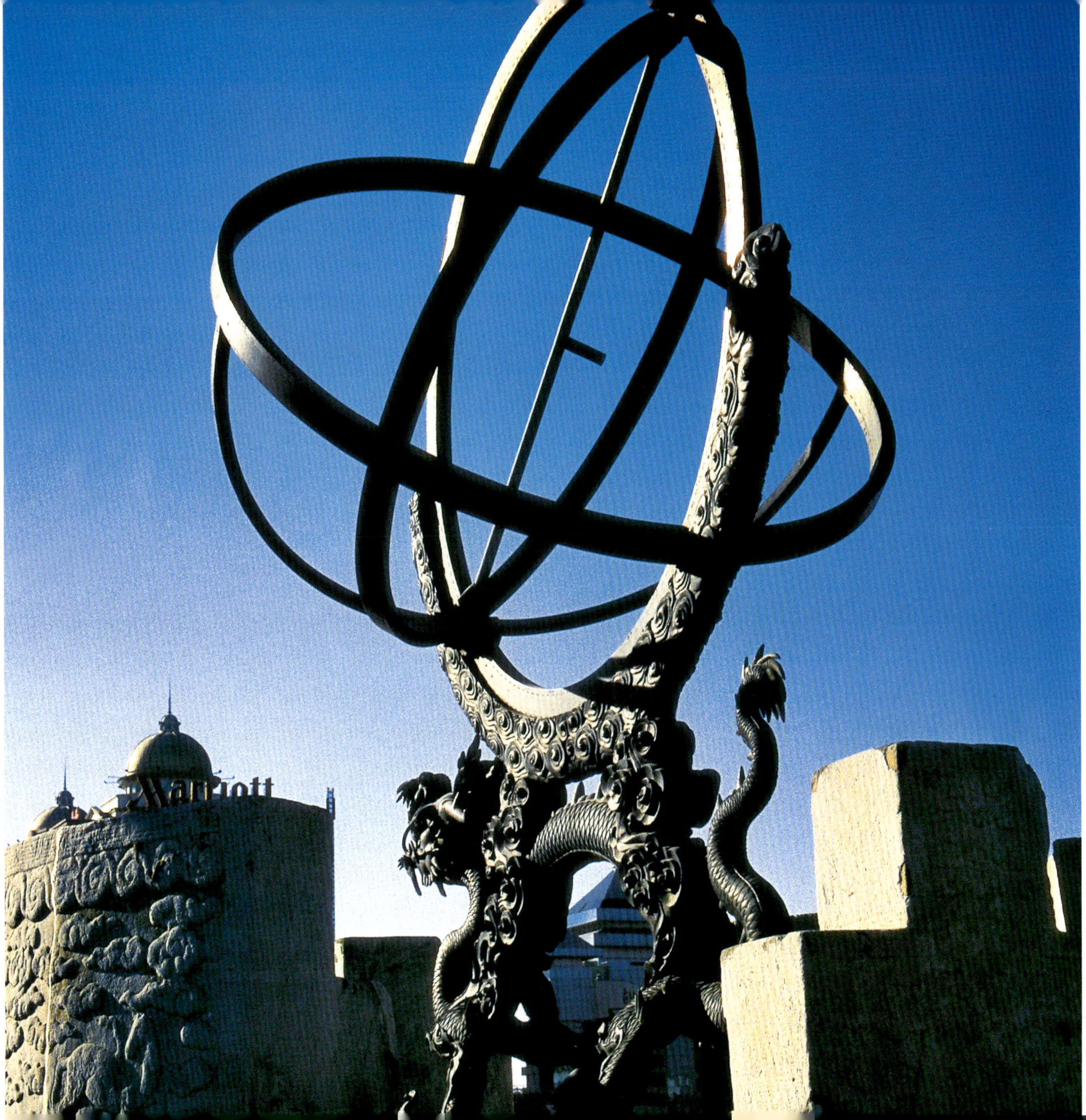

北京猿人遗址
Peking Man Ruins

位于北京西南郊的周口店。1929年12月，人类学家在周口店的一个山洞里发现了生活在距今70万～20万年之间，能直立行走、会制造工具、会使用火的北京猿人化石，以及他们的生活痕迹。

Zhoukoudian in southwest Beijing was where the traces of Peking Man were discovered in December 1929. Peking Man lived some 700,000-200,000 years ago. They could walk erectly, make tools and use fire.

延庆古崖居
Guyaju Ancient Caves

古崖居位于北京西北延庆山区峡谷中，共有 117 个洞穴。它是目前北京地区发现的规模最大的古代先民洞窟聚落遗址，何人开凿、开凿年代和用途至今仍是一个谜。

Guyaju has 117 ancient caves in the mountains of Yanqing in northwest Beijing. No one can tell who had dug these caves, and when and why.

明城墙遗址
Ruins of Ming City Wall

在崇文门与东便门之间，有一段已有 500 余年历史的明城墙。这是北京明清古城墙中仅存的一部分，2002 年，北京市将这里修建成开放式的明城墙遗址公园。

Stretching between Chongwenmen and Dongbianmen is a short section and the only ruins of the 500-year-old Ming Dynasty city wall.

菖蒲河公园
Changpu River Park

菖蒲河也称外金水河，源自皇城西苑中海，流经天安门前，沿皇城南墙内汇入御河，现辟为菖蒲河公园。

Changpu River, or Outer Golden River, originates from the western hills and runs past Tian'anmen Rostrum to the east. Now, there is a park built along the river.

菖蒲河公园鸟瞰 Changpu River Park

从塔身的辽代浮雕人们可以解读辽代的艺术风格
The relief on the pagoda was of typical Liao style.

天宁寺古塔
Tianning Temple Pagoda

天宁寺是北京市现存年代最久远的佛寺，距今约有1500余年的历史。寺院内的辽代砖塔始建于1083年，为仿木结构的密檐实心砖塔，高57.8米，造型及塔身雕塑极为精美。（右图）

The 1,500-year Tianning Temple is the oldest extant temple in Beijing. The 57.8-meter-high brick pagoda was first built in 1083 and looks very beautiful with intricate brick carvings and close layers of eaves.

五塔寺
Five Pagoda Temple

五塔寺原名真觉寺，始建于明代永乐年间(1403-1424年)，现在是北京石刻艺术馆所在地。寺内的金刚宝座塔模仿印度中早期佛塔样式建造，塔身遍布宗教题材的精美雕刻。（右页图）

Five Pagoda Temple was built during 1403-1424. The five Indian-style pagodas bear religious carvings. Now this is the location of Beijing Museum of Stone Carvings Art.

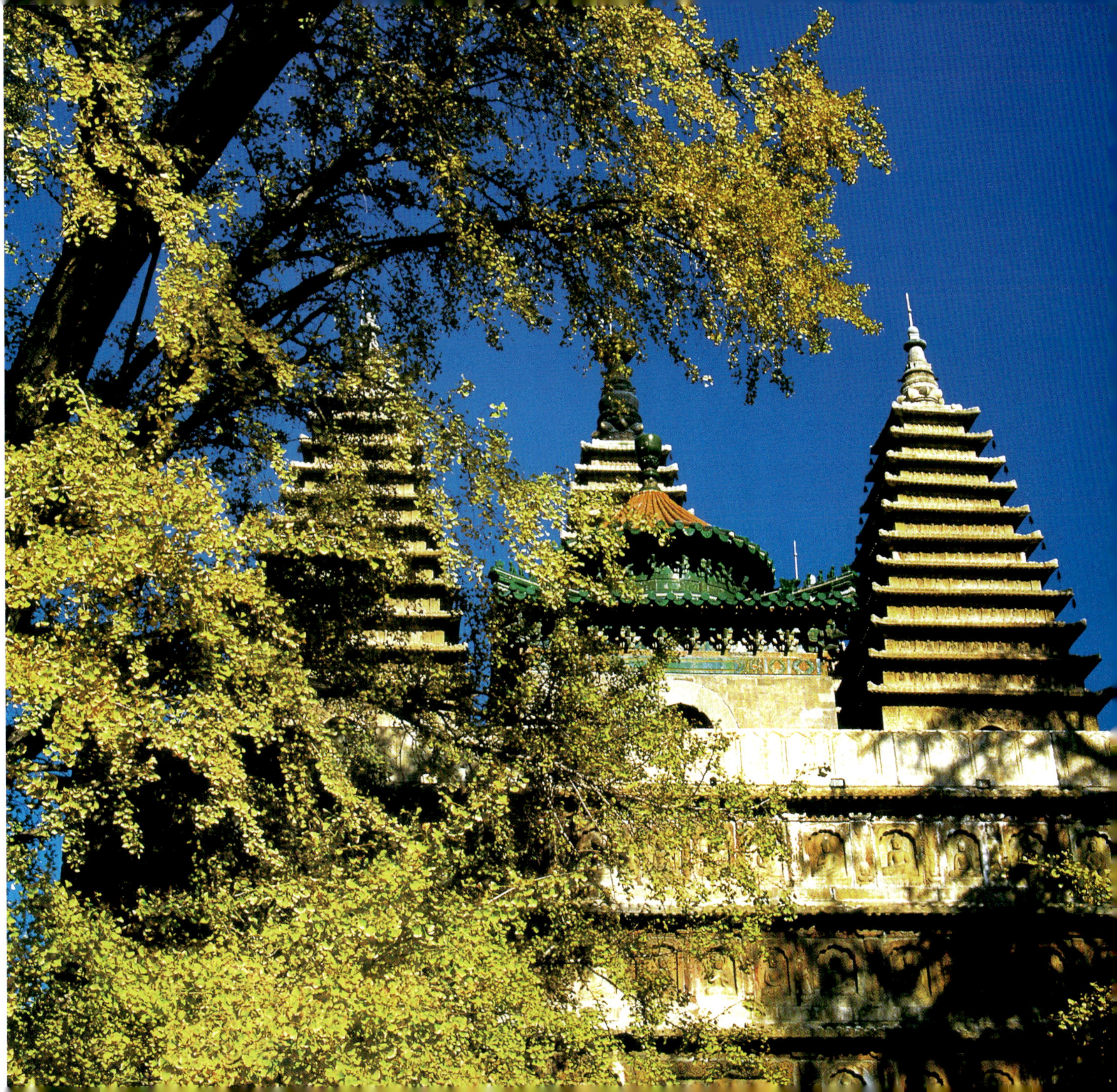

京味文化
BEIJING CULTURE

许多到北京旅游的人，都喜欢逛北京的胡同，尝北京的烤鸭和小吃，听北京的京剧，甚至到公园里和自娱自乐的"老北京"一起唱上几段戏，觉得那才是品味了京味文化。

到底什么是京味文化呢？京味文化是指以原来的北京内城为根基，带有明显的北京地区特色的文学、艺术、建筑、语言、民俗以及处世哲学等内容的文化现象，其特点是兼容并蓄、宽厚平和、幽默达观。而要品味、体验京味文化，最好的方式是走进胡同，近距离接触北京居民的生活。如果有时间，那就背上照相机，迈开双腿，走进胡同、走进街巷，去体验京味文化的魅力吧。

Visitors to Beijing prefer to stroll in hutong, try some local snacks or roast duck, listen to Peking opera, or even join the locals to sing one or two lines. This is the best way to experience and enjoy the local culture.

The typical features of local culture are the ease and humorous lifestyle and broad mind of the people.

故宫角楼与景山
A corner tower at the Palace Museum and Jingshan

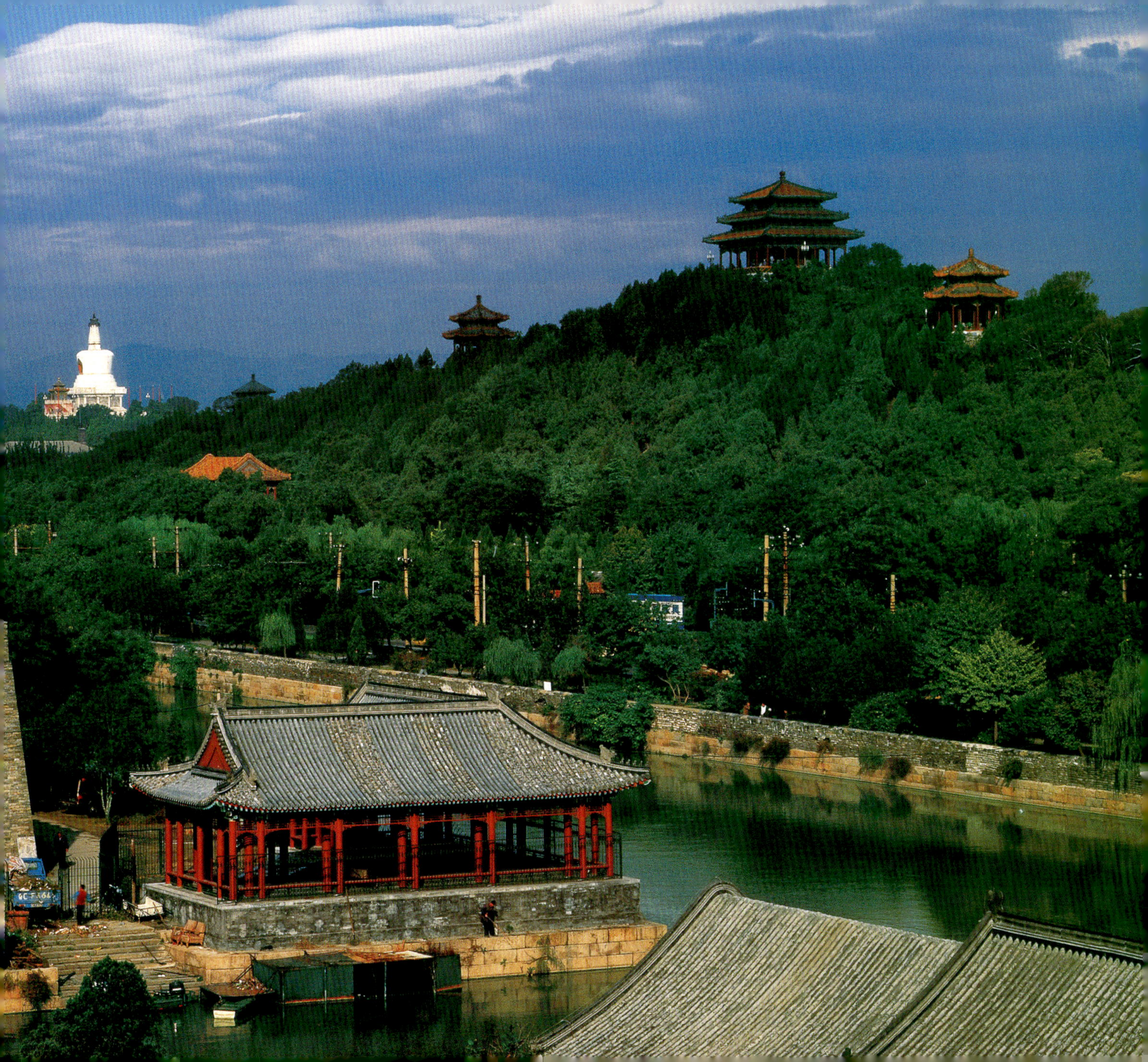

什刹海景区
Shichahai Lakes

位于北京市中心的什刹海地区，是老北京四合院保留区，由前海、后海、西海三个湖泊组成，夏天碧波粼粼，柳翠荷香；冬天冰平如镜，是天然的滑冰场。沿岸分布着保存完好的清朝皇亲贵戚居住的王府以及普通老百姓的民居，雕梁画栋与灰墙黛瓦和谐相处，高贵典雅中蕴涵着质朴平和。近几年，什刹海地区吸引了许多各种风格的酒吧、餐馆和特色商店在这里经营，成为北京城既有老北京风情，又有新时尚气息的游览、休闲胜地。

Shichahai, to the north of Beihai Park, is made up of three lakes. In summer, the breeze wafts the lotus scent, while in winter, the lakes form a natural skating rink for the locals, young and old. Along the lakes are many well-preserved siheyuan courtyard houses, some once being residences of royal princes. The richly painted beams coexist with the plain gray walls, a pleasant combination of grandness and simplicity. In recent years, a bunch of bustling bars, restaurants and boutiques have settled here, making the Shichahai area a hangout place with both old charms and latest fashions.

银锭桥位于什刹海的前海和后海之间的水道上，是一座单孔石拱桥。据说过去人们站在银锭桥上可遥望西山，是为清代"燕京八景"之一的"银锭观山"。1984年，原桥拆除重建，仍以"银锭桥"为名。

Yinding Bridge got its name from its shape of a silver ingot. It's said that in old times when there was no high-rise, one could see the western hills standing on this lovely single-arch stone bridge. The original bridge was renovated in 1984.

钟鼓楼是古代的报时工具，晨钟暮鼓伴随着老北京人度过了数百年的岁月。

The Tower of Drum and Bell, ancient timekeeping structures, have witnessed tremendous changes over the centuries.

胡同
Hutong

　　自元大都开始，北京城有了胡同。在七八百年间，胡同构成了北京城的基本骨架。北京到底有多少条胡同？老北京人说：有名的胡同三千六，没名的胡同数不清。

Hutong was a Mongolian word for "alley". Hutong began to be built in the Yuan Dynasty when Beijing was called Dadu. In the following 700-800 years, numerous hutong formed the urban framework of Beijing. How many hutong are there in Beijing? Senior locals may answer: 3,600 famous ones, and countless unknown ones.

胡同里的一个个由院墙围合而成的四合院就是北京人的传统住宅。
The courtyards built along hutong are called siheyuan, traditional living quarters for local residents.

门墩是四合院建筑的特色之一。
Mendun(stone block supporting the pivot of a door) is a typical feature of siheyuan resdence.

坐上三轮车,在曲折蜿蜒的胡同里漫游、到四合院里尝尝老北京的饺子,是最受旅游者欢迎的"北京胡同游"。
A tour through the narrow, winding hutong on pedicabs and a taste of stuffed dumplings done with the siheyuan residents are most enjoyable to visitors from around the world.

前门大街
Qianmen Street

前门大街正对着昔日的皇城，当年是京城繁华的商业街市。前门大街有多家老字号商店，至今仍是百姓喜爱的购物场所。

Qianmen Street which leads directly to the former imperial palace and dotted with some old stores is still a popular shopping center in the city today.

明清两朝的皇城中轴线从南城的永定门到北城的钟鼓楼,全长7.8公里,是古都北京的城市建设中心和标志,也是目前世界上最长的城市中轴线。

In the Ming and Qing dynasties, the axis of the city extended 7.8 kilometers from the Yongding Gate in the south to the Bell and Drum Towers in the north. The axis is an important geographical mark of Beijing, and the ancient capital was built around this world's longest city axis.

京剧
Peking Opera

北京是被外国人称为"北京歌剧"的国粹——京剧的故乡。京剧有200余年的历史，起源于几种古老的地方戏剧，18世纪末开始在北京发展、形成。京剧集歌、舞、念、打、音、美、文于一体，逐渐成为上至皇室、下至百姓，雅俗共赏的"国剧"。如今，北京既有长安大戏院这样的豪华剧场，也有梅兰芳大剧院、前门梨园剧场和湖广会馆古戏楼这样的特色戏院。这些地方经常上演精彩的传统剧目和新编剧目。在北京的各大公园里，更随时可以看到一群群操琴打板、自得其乐地唱着京剧的北京人。

Beijing is the hometown of the 200-year-old Peking Opera. Peking Opera was developed on the basis of several operas popular in other places. It took its form in Beijing in late the 18th century, and blended singing, dancing, reciting, acrobatics, music and fine arts. It was popular among both common people and imperial families. Today, traditional and newly revised operas are presented at Chang'an Grand Theater, Mei Lanfang Theater, Liyuan Theater and Huguang Guildhall. For self-entertainment, many fans enjoy themselves by singing Peking Opera in parks.

演出前，演员在后台勾脸。勾好的脸叫做脸谱。用脸谱表现各种人物是京剧的一大特点。

Before going to the stage, the performers will draw their makeup backstage. Different types of characters have different makeup.

湖广会馆位于京味文化的起源地城南宣武区，始建于清嘉庆十二年（1807年），经常上演京剧的经典剧目。

Huguang Guildhall in Xuanwu District was first built in 1807. It is the right place to enjoy repertoire Peking Opera.

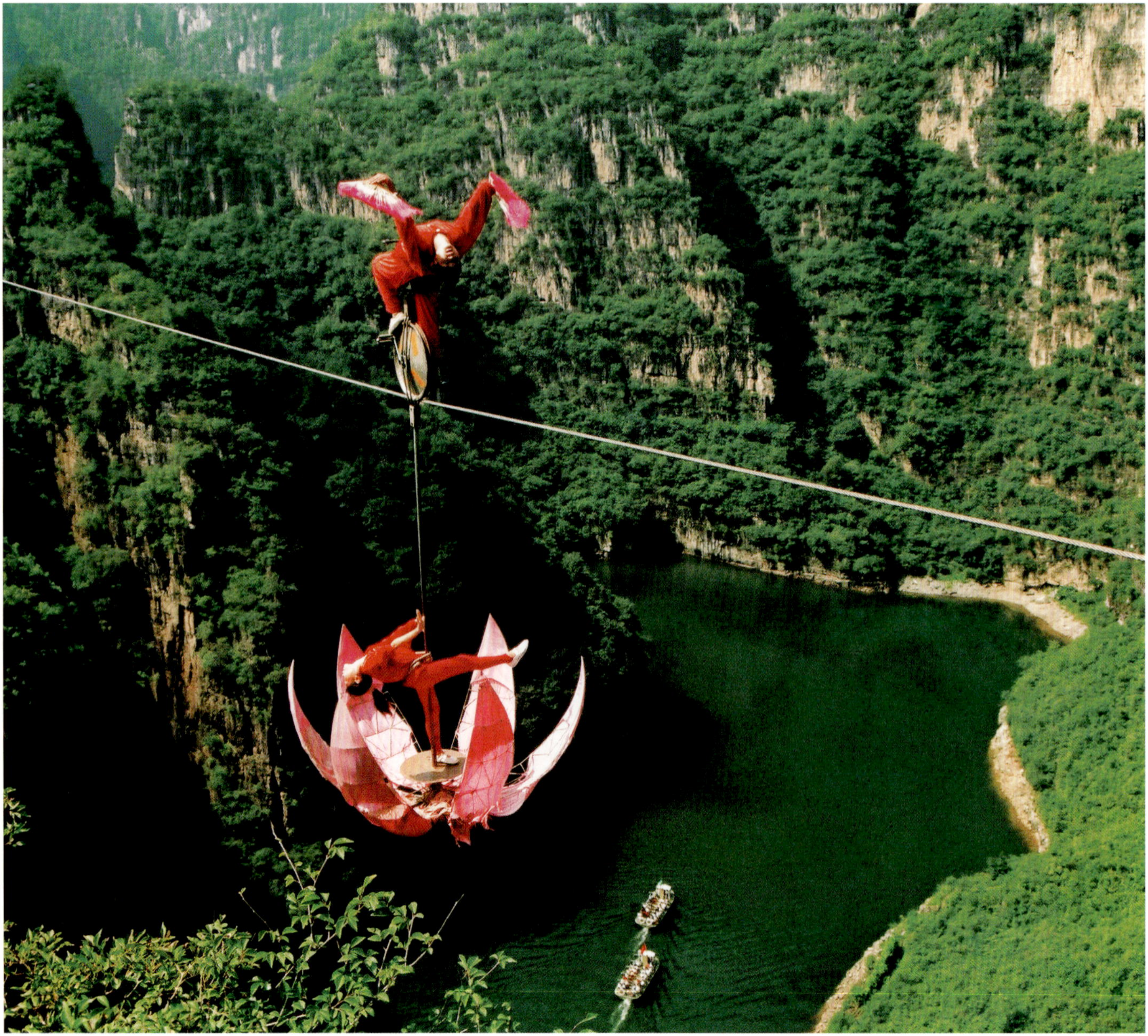

杂技
Acrobatics

　　北京的魅力在于文化生活的丰富多彩,北京不仅是外来艺术充分展示的舞台,民族传统艺术也得到了很好的传承。中国的杂技世界闻名,在北京能欣赏到世界一流的杂技表演,《椅子顶》、《转碟》、《走钢丝》、《抖空竹》等杂技节目是地地道道的、精湛的民间传统艺术。

The charm of Beijing lies in its rich cultural life. While presenting external arts, traditional art forms such as acrobatics are also well preserved. Chinese acrobatics is known in the world. In Beijing, one can appreciate first class acrobatic performances like Chair Tip, Rotating Dishes, Steel Wire Walking and Hollow Bamboo Playing.

民俗曲艺
Folk Arts

踩高跷是传统的民间技艺。人站在一根细细的木棍上行走,惊险刺激。(左上图)
Walking on high sticks often attracts a large audience.

流传了数百年的皮影戏依然受到孩子们的喜爱。(左下图)
The centuries-old puppet show still popular with today's children.

老北京民间曲艺双簧表演幽默风趣。(右图)
Two-man comic show with one speaking or singing behind the other who gesticulates.

在喜庆的时刻舞狮、舞龙是包括北京在内的中国民间传统风俗。由人来舞动，模仿龙或者狮子的游动、跳跃，以烘托喜庆的气氛。

Dragon and lion dances are among the folk activities on festivals. The performers mime the movements of dragon and lion to add lively atmosphere.

97

琉璃厂古文化街
Liulichang Antiques Street

  体验京味文化不要忘了去逛逛古文化街琉璃厂，那里也是最有北京特色的地方。琉璃厂位于和平门外大街，形成于大约200年前。琉璃厂曾经是中国传统字画、文房四宝、古旧书籍展示和交易的一个特定场所。现在，这条仿古的文化街是喜爱中国传统文化的中外游客和文化人"淘金"的好地方。

  One must not miss Liulichang if he is to explore local culture. Some 200 years ago, Liulichang became a trade center for Chinese paintings and calligraphy works, four treasures in study and old books. Today, Liulichang is a" gold mine" for both tourists and those who love traditional Chinese culture.

北京是多民族聚居区，不同民族的节庆也就成了北京的节日。当然，北京最重要的节日是春节。

春节是中国农历新年，也是中华民族的传统节日。除夕之夜，传统是要全家团圆，包饺子、吃团圆饭。春节期间，各种类型的庙会上有许多民间艺术表演和让人垂涎的各种小吃，闻风而动的风车、一米多长的大糖葫芦是只有春节才能见到的北京民俗产品。

Beijing is a gathering place of various ethnic groups. Different ethnic groups have different festivals. Spring Festival is the most important festival in Beijing.

Spring Festival is the Chinese lunar New Year. On the eve, the whole family gather to make dumplings and have dinner together. During the Spring Festival, temple fairs will be organized, where the locals can watch folk art performances and enjoy various snacks. Huge windmills and sugarcoated haws on a stick as long as one meter are exclusively for the festival.

糖葫芦是最具北京地方特色的小吃，老人小孩儿都喜爱。
Tanghulu, or sugar coated haws, is a local snack favored by many, young and old.

北京烤鸭
Beijing Roast Duck

　　无论是外地游客还是外国游客，到了北京有一道美味不能不尝，这就是烤鸭。北京最著名的烤鸭店叫"全聚德"。这家老字号创建于130年前，其用挂炉方式烤制的烤鸭皮脆肉嫩，外表色泽鲜艳。现在，"全聚德"的连锁店已开到了外省和外国。另一家老字号烤鸭店叫"便宜坊"，以焖炉烤鸭为招牌。两家烤鸭各有特色，都是美味，所以，小小烤鸭居然成为北京风味餐饮的代表。

　　Roast duck is a must for visitors to Beijing. The most popular roast duck restaurant is Quanjude, which has operated for over 130 years. Now it has many chain restaurants across China and the world. Another old roast duck restaurant is Bianyifang. Roast ducks served at these two restaurants are slightly different in terms of flavor, but all taste good.

三元桥
Sanyuan overpass

现代都市
MODERN METROPOLIS

　　北京作为历史文化名城而闻名中外,她像一座巨大的博物馆典藏着中华民族的悠久历史和灿烂文化。但是,北京又是一座非常现代化的都市,她的前进步伐紧扣着全球社会与经济发展的节奏。五十余年来,北京已经从一个纯粹的消费城市演变为一个社会发展和经济总量在全中国名列前茅的现代化大都市,成为全中国人民向往的地方和闻名遐迩的旅游胜地。

　　Beijing is a historical and cultural city. It is also a modern city keeping abreast of the pace of global social and economic development. In 50 years, Beijing has grown from a pure consuming city into a modern metropolis that leads others in China in cultural, economic and technological development. It is also a tourist magnet.

中关村
Zhongguancun

　　中关村科技园区是中国第一家高科技园区,其软件、集成电路、计算机、网络、通信等重点产业集群带动了首都经济结构调整和产业升级。

　　Zhongguancun Science Park is the first of its kind in China. Its software, integrate circuit, computer, network and communications have greatly boosted Beijing's economic restructuring and industrial upgrading.

中央电视塔
CCTV Tower

中央电视塔总高405米，塔旁一条碧水流过，风景如画。
Pleasant scenery around the 405-meter-high CCTV Tower and the artificial canal flowing by.

国际贸易中心曾是北京的外资和合资公司最多、商务最繁忙的地方，如今，以国贸中心为基点的北京CBD商务中心区拔地而起，标示着北京作为现代商务城市的一个侧面。
World Trade Center, gathering the most foreign-funded or joint-ventures, is the busiest place in Beijing. The Central Business District, centering on the World Trade Center, is a new landmark of Beijing.

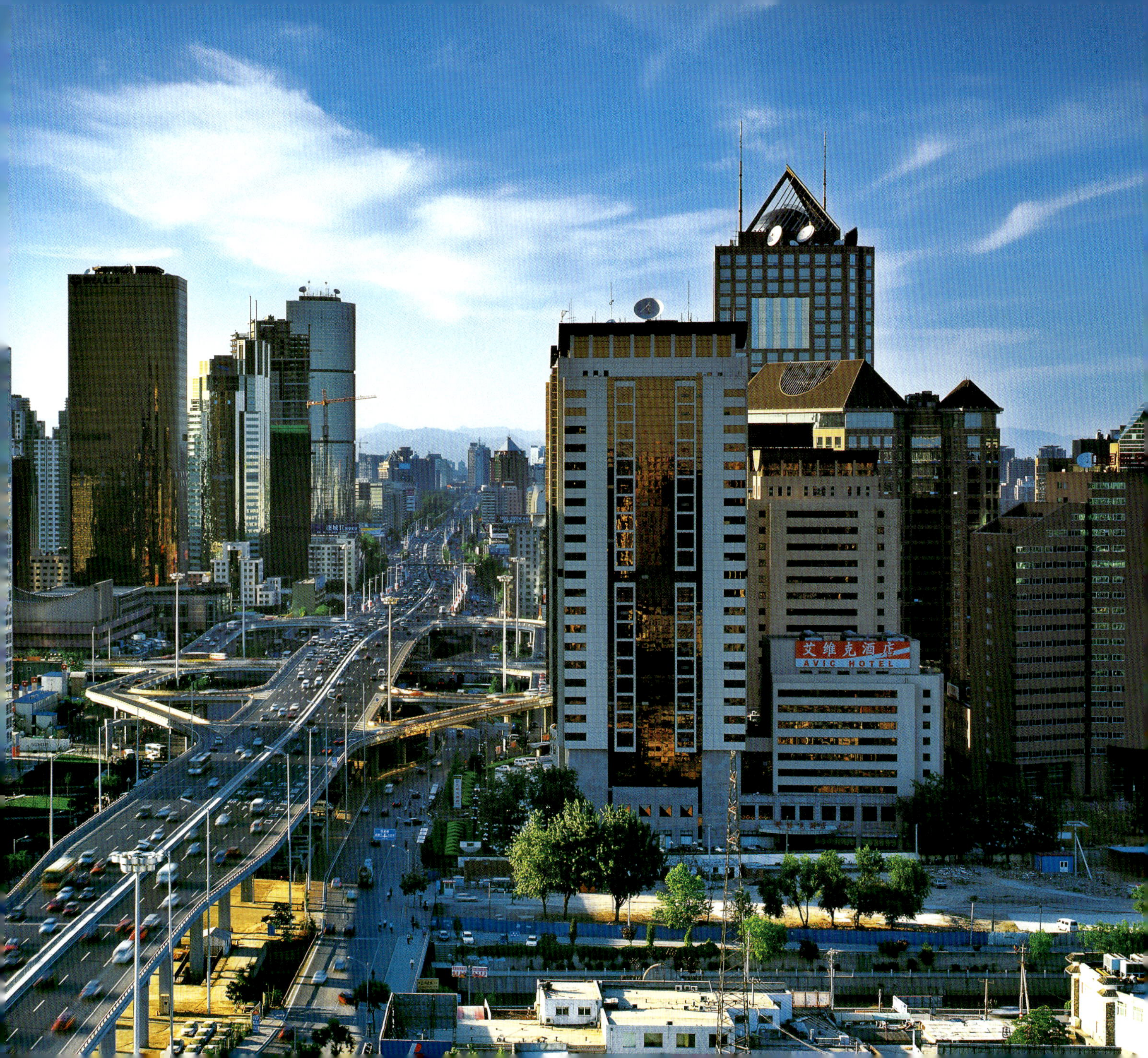
艾维克酒店
AVIC HOTEL

与"金街"王府井比肩而立的东方广场时尚、现代。
The Orient Plaza by Wangfujing Street is a center of fashion.

北京,一个正在走向现代化的古老城市,在努力保护传统的同时,也非常注重吸收新的理念。旧与新、历史与现代在这个城市和谐并存。

Old and new coexist in Beijing, a centuries-old city that welcomes new ideas while protecting traditions.

"秀水街"是早年紧邻使馆区的一条狭长小街，以经营外贸服装、丝绸制品和旅游纪念品而出名。新建的秀水街市场成为建筑面积达28000平方米的商城，有上千个摊位，经营方式仍然保留着当年的特色。

Silk Alley was once a narrow lane, crowded with Chinese and foreigners coming for garments, silk products and tourist souvenirs. Today, bargaining is still the fashion in the new shopping building erecting on the former alley, with 28,000 square meters of floor area and over 1,000 stalls.

王府井
Wangfujing

"金街"王府井是北京最著名的商业街，到北京的人没有不去王府井大街逛逛的。2000年改造成步行街后，突出了王府井的历史和文化内涵。如今，"金街"白天人群熙攘，夜晚灯火辉煌，一片热闹景象。

Wangfujing is the bustling commercial street in Beijing. After renovation in 2000, the street emphasizes more of its historical and cultural contents. The" Golden Street" is crowded with people during the day and luminous and bustling at night.

中国科学技术馆
China Science and Technology Museum

中国科学技术馆1988年9月建成开放，汇集了中国古代科技和现代科技的精华，功能包括展览教育、培训教育、实验教育，鼓励公众在参观过程中亲自动手探索与实践。

The China Science and Technology Museum was completed and opened to visitors in September 1988. It displays ancient and modern Chinese science and technology. Visitors can have a try in the experiment.

首都博物馆
Capital Museum

首都博物馆新馆，2006年5月在西长安街建成开放。其外观和内部设计既充满浓郁的民族特色，又有鲜明的现代感。新馆的展览陈列以历年收藏和北京地区的出土文物为主要内容，吸收相关学科的最新研究成果，形成独具北京文化特色的现代化展陈。

The new Capital Museum on west Chang'an Avenue opened to the public in May 2006. It features relics unearthed in the Beijing area, which can be seen from both its out appearance and interior layout.

中华世纪坛
China Millennium Monument

为迎接21世纪的到来，北京建设了纪念性建筑中华世纪坛，以展示中华民族光辉灿烂的文化，弘扬中华民族的伟大精神为主题。

中华世纪坛世纪大厅环形壁画和回廊间雕塑的设计，体现出深厚的华夏文化内涵以及中国人对民族复兴的自信与豪情。

The China Millennium Monument was built to greet the 21st century and the new millennium. It hosts exhibitions of both vernacular and exotic cultures.

The circular fresco and sculptures in the lobby depict the cream of Chinese civilization and the pride of the Chinese nation.

798 艺术园区
798 Art District

798艺术园区曾是20世纪50年代至80年代大型国有电子企业集中的工业区。2002年开始，一些年轻的中国艺术家利用废弃的厂房改建成独立工作室，进行绘画、雕塑等艺术品的创作和展览。798艺术园区作为北京最有创造力与代表性的新的文化现象正在引起世人的注意。

在798艺术园区，不同年代最有创造力和代表性的艺术作品展示着中国艺术的发展历程。

The 798 art district used to be the grounds of state-owned electronic factories in the 1950s to 1980s. Starting in 2002, some young Chinese artists have turned the abandoned workshops into painting or sculpture studios. Now, 798 has become a cultural phenomenon representing the dynamic creativity of Beijing.

The art works of different styles and representing different eras in China together record the evolution course of Chinese art.

国家大剧院

National Center for the Performing Arts

　　由法国著名建筑师设计,2007年投入使用的国家大剧院外形是一个巨大、独特的壳体,高46.68米,建筑造型简约现代,内部装饰华美典雅,与附近中国古典风格的建筑相映成辉。大剧院内设有歌剧院、音乐厅和戏剧场等专业剧场。在大剧院欣赏高雅艺术如今是北京人的新享受。

　　The National Center for the Performing Arts, designed by a French architect, came into operation in 2007. It has an opera house, a concert hall and a theater.

现代城市交通
Urban Traffic

2007年10月投入运营的地铁5号线设计理念先进，贯通京城南北，与正在建设中的地铁10号线、4号线、9号线，以及运营中的1号线、2号线、八通线、城铁13号线等，在北京城的地下"编织"出一张巨大的公共交通网。到2015年，北京的轨道交通总里程将达到561公里，更加方便人们的工作与生活。

Beijing is China's largest hub of air, railway and highway transportation.

Subway Line 5, coming into operation in October 2007, runs north-south through the city to link up three other lines (10, 4 and 9) still under construction, and the operating Lines 1 and 2, Batong Line and Light Rail 13. They form an underground traffic network. By 2015, Beijing's subways will extend 561 kilometers.

德胜门是老北京城九门之一，古老的城楼与现代化的公路网和谐并存。
Co-existence of ancient building and modern highway at Desheng Gate, one of the nine gates to the ancient capital.

首都国际机场
Capital International Airport

　　首都国际机场是中国最大的航空枢纽和民用航空网络的辐射中心。现在，首都国际机场是中国第一个拥有三座航站楼、双塔台、三条跑道同时运营的机场，旅客年吞吐设计总量达到8200万人次，跻身世界前十大最繁忙机场行列。

　　Beijing Capital International Airport is the largest air transportation hub in China. It is one of the world's 10 busiest airports, with three terminal buildings, two control towers and three runways, and handling 82 million passengers a year.

四通八达的立交桥构成了现代北京的交通网络。
Cloverleaves link modern Beijing and have formed a transportation network in the city.

2008 奥运场馆
2008 Olympic Arenas

2008年8月在北京举行的第29届奥运会为这个古老而充满活力的城市勾画出了更加美好的前景。"绿色奥运、科技奥运、人文奥运"是北京古城为从雅典古城远道而来的人类和平圣火备下的"盛宴"。北京，伴随着奥运会的步伐，进入了以和谐、文明、环保、绿色为理念的发展新阶段。

The 29th Olympics scheduled in August 2008 surely brings great opportunities for Beijing, and this old city full of vigor is ready to present the world a grand event:" Green Olympics, High-Tech Olympics and People's Olympics".

北京工人体育场建成于 1959 年 8 月，是当年北京著名的十大建筑之一。为迎接 2008 年奥运会，工人体育场进行了全面改造，重新焕发了青春活力，成为可容纳 62000 名观众的奥运足球场。

Beijing Workers' Stadium was completed in August 1958 as one of the 10 great projects in Beijing then. Large overhaul brings it new outlook and modern outfit to accommodate 62,000 audience.

国家游泳中心是一座占地面积近 8 万平方米的蓝色水晶方盒子式建筑。她被人们形象地称为"水立方",是由海外华人华侨自愿捐资修建的 2008 年北京奥运会游泳、跳水及花样游泳比赛场馆。

National Aquatics Center, or Watercube, is a blue crystal-like box covering nearly 80,000 square meters of land. It was built with the donations from overseas Chinese for the swimming, diving and synchronizes swimming competition in 2008.

因造型酷似"鸟巢"而得名的国家体育场位于北京奥林匹克公园中心区南部,是2008年第29届奥林匹克运动会的主体育场。主体建筑为巨型空间马鞍形钢桁架编织式结构,场内观众坐席约有9.1万个。

The National Stadium, nicknamed Bird's Nest for its shape, is located in the south of the Olympic Park. It is the main arena of the 2008 Olympics and can accommodate 91,000 audience.

进入21世纪，北京的发展更为迅速、和谐。如果您与北京素未谋面，欢迎您来探访这座谜一般的城市；如果您来过北京，请您再来看看这座日新月异的东方名城。

夕阳西下，两个少年正骑着自行车穿过昔日皇城的大门。北京如同这两个少年一样，从悠长的历史隧道走来，带着新的希望，向着美好的未来快步前进。

Beijing is changing even swifter in the 21st century. It welcomes, as always, visitors from around the world to have an experience of its profound history and modern outlook.

As the two boys ride past the centuries-old gate of the former imperial palace, they enter a world for discovery. So is Beijing, a city laden with ancient memories and a brighter future.